At Issue

Childhood Obesity

Tamara Thompson, Book Editor

GREENHAVEN PRESS
A part of Gale, Cengage Learning

GALE
CENGAGE Learning·

Farmington Hills, Mich • San Francisco • New York • Waterville, Maine
Meriden, Conn • Mason, Ohio • Chicago

Judy Galens, *Manager, Frontlist Acquisitions*

© 2016 Greenhaven Press, a part of Gale, Cengage Learning.

Gale and Greenhaven Press are registered trademarks used herein under license.

For more information, contact:
Greenhaven Press
27500 Drake Rd.
Farmington Hills, MI 48331-3535
Or you can visit our Internet site at gale.cengage.com

For product information and technology assistance, contact us at

Gale Customer Support, 1-800-877-4253
For permission to use material from this text or product, submit all requests online at www.cengage.com/permissions

Further permissions questions can be e-mailed to permissionrequest@cengage.com

Articles in Greenhaven Press anthologies are often edited for length to meet page requirements. In addition, original titles of these works are changed to clearly present the main thesis and to explicitly indicate the author's opinion. Every effort is made to ensure that Greenhaven Press accurately reflects the original intent of the authors. Every effort has been made to trace the owners of copyrighted material.

Cover image © Images.com/Corbis.

LIBRARY OF CONGRESS CATALOGING-IN-PUBLICATION DATA

Childhood obesity / Tamara Thompson, book editor.
    pages cm. -- (At issue)
Includes bibliographical references and index.
    ISBN 978-0-7377-7404-7 (hardcover) -- ISBN 978-0-7377-7405-4 (pbk.)
1. Obesity in children. I. Thompson, Tamara.
    RJ399.C6C47213 2016
    618.92'398--dc23
                                                        2015024555

Printed in the United States of America
    1 2 3 4 5   19 18 17 16 15

Contents

Introduction

When Michelle Obama, in Spring 2009, planted a sprawling vegetable garden on the White House grounds for the first time since Eleanor Roosevelt's World War II "victory garden," it was the start of what became a signature cause for the First Lady: combating childhood obesity.

Now an annual planting tradition, the so-called Kitchen Garden does more than just provide fresh produce for the Obamas and their guests; it is also a highly visible platform to educate Americans about the benefits of a healthy diet.

"Our White House Kitchen Garden has bloomed into so much more," wrote Obama in her 2012 book, *American Grown*. "It's helped us start a new conversation about the food we eat and how it affects our children's health. It's helped us raise awareness about our crisis of childhood obesity and the threat it poses to our children's future. And it led to the creation of Let's Move!, a nationwide initiative to solve this problem so our children can grow up healthy."[1]

The First Lady's motivation for picking childhood obesity as her cause to champion was personal; her daughters' pediatrician had taken her aside and expressed concern about the girls' weight and diet, something she had not even noticed was a problem.

The Obamas are not alone in overlooking potential weight problems in their children. According to recent research reported in *The New York Times*, most parents think their kids are at a proper weight even when they are clinically obese,

---

1. Michelle Obama, *American Grown: The Story of the White House Kitchen Garden and Gardens Across America*. New York: Crown, 2012.

meaning they are not just overweight for their height but also at risk of developing health problems from having too much body fat.[2]

Two-thirds of adults and one in three American children are considered overweight or obese, and childhood obesity has more than tripled since 1980. Today, more than twelve million children and teens are obese and more than twenty-three million are either obese or overweight, a third of the under-eighteen population; the numbers are even higher in Native American, Black, and Hispanic communities. Health officials say childhood obesity has now reached an epidemic proportion and is the biggest threat to children's health since polio in the 1950s.

Obesity statistics are more than just numbers, however; they translate into very real health consequences for very real people. Medical professionals are alarmed by the number of obese children who are developing serious medical conditions usually only seen in adults, such as type 2 diabetes, high blood pressure, and atherosclerosis (hardening of the arteries). Children who are obese face increased risks for heart disease, strokes, asthma, arthritis, and even cancers over the course of their lives. A third of all children born in the year 2000 can expect to develop diabetes during their lifetimes, and they can expect to live shorter lives as well; children who are obese are more than twice as likely to die before age fifty-five than children who are a healthy weight.

As Jacob Warren and K. Bryant Smalley explain in their recent book, *Always the Fat Kid*, the average life expectancy for today's generation of American children is shorter than the preceding generation for the first time ever. The unprecedented decrease "has been attributed nearly entirely to the staggering rates of childhood obesity" and the various health

2. KJ Dell'Antonia, "Parents Don't Notice Extra Pounds on Overweight Children," *New York Times*, May 20, 2015. http://parenting.blogs.nytimes.com/2015/05/20/parents -dont-notice-extra-pounds-on-overweight-children/.

risks and diseases associated with it.[3] Obesity is currently estimated to cause 112,000 deaths each year in the United States, a figure that will continue to grow as today's obese children become tomorrow's obese adults, as 80 percent are expected to do.

The economic consequences of such a shift are just as formidable as the physical consequences. As reported by Michelle Healy in *USA Today*, researchers at the Duke Global Health Institute and Duke-NUS Graduate Medical School in Singapore recently determined that over the course of a lifetime direct medical costs associated with childhood obesity run about $19,000 per child.[4] Childhood obesity is estimated to cause $14.3 billion in medical costs each year, and an estimated 21 percent of all US health-care spending is currently obesity related.

The Robert Wood Johnson Foundation estimates that if the child obesity trend continues, by 2022 obesity rates for adults could reach or exceed 44 percent nationwide and 60 percent in more than a dozen states; type 2 diabetes and other obesity-related ailments could increase tenfold between 2010 and 2020 and then double again by 2030; and obesity-related health-care costs—already some $190 billion a year—could increase 10 to 20 percent nationwide.[5]

Although the physical and economic costs of childhood obesity seem readily apparent, the causes of the epidemic itself are less so. Long viewed as an individual character failing or the result of poor parenting, many experts now consider childhood obesity to be a societal problem caused by a host of fac-

3. Jacob Warren and K. Bryant Smalley, *Always the Fat Kid: The Truth About the Enduring Effects of Childhood Obesity.* New York: Palgrave McMillan, 2013, p. 27.

4. Michelle Healy, "Price Tag for Childhood Obesity: $19,000 per Kid," *USA Today,* April 7, 2014. http://www.usatoday.com/story/news/nation/2014/04/07/childhood-obesity -costs/7298461.

5. Jeffrey Levi et al., "F as in Fat: How Obesity Threatens America's Future 2012," Robert Wood Johnson Foundation and Trust for America's Health, September 2012. http:// www.rwjf.org/en/library/research/2012/09/f-as-in-fat--how-obesity-threatens-america -s-future-2012.html.

tors that work in synergy to create an "obesogenic" culture—one that promotes weight gain and in which being overweight or obese is hard to avoid.

Obesity experts point to the wide availability of cheap, highly processed foods that are high in fat, sugar, and salt; aggressive junk food marketing that targets children; the supersizing of fast food meals and sodas; and "food deserts" where there is limited access to fresh foods as some of the factors that have increased the number of calories children consume each day.

At the same time that children are eating more, they are also moving their bodies less and burning fewer calories. Instead of outdoor activities, play for most kids now consists of sedentary time spent in front of a screen, playing video games, texting with friends, or watching entertainment media. Modern safety concerns make it more likely that parents drive their kids to school rather than letting them walk or bike, and many urban communities simply lack safe places for children to play or exercise.

It is precisely these issues—the limited availability of healthy foods and not enough exercise—that are the focus of the First Lady's Let's Move! program, as well as that of the White House Task Force on Child Obesity, which works to develop public policies to reduce childhood obesity.

But not everyone agrees that childhood obesity is a problem, let alone one that warrants government intervention. Critics complain that antiobesity efforts represent the "nanny state" at its worst and are an example of government overreach and encroachment into the prerogatives of parenting.

Indeed, there has been sharp backlash for some of the recent policies aimed at reducing childhood obesity. New federal school lunch nutrition standards have been widely lambasted, with photos of pathetic-looking student lunches going viral online; parents have cried foul over rules limiting the amount of juice a toddler can have at day care; the food and beverage industry has rejected the idea of voluntary guidelines to limit food marketing to children; and the philosophical argument has been raised that the government should not be in the business of dictating what people eat.

Meanwhile, others argue that antiobesity efforts are counterproductive because they put undue emphasis on appearance and that people who eat healthfully, exercise regularly, and feel good about themselves, regardless of their weight, are indeed healthy, a principle known as "health at every size."

As Laura Dawes explains in her 2014 book, *Childhood Obesity in America*, "the fat acceptance movement argues that the medicalization of obesity is just one symptom of a groundless 'moral panic' about fat—a situation that is promoted by the self-serving interests of the diet, fashion, pharmaceutical, and cosmetic industries, and by obesity researchers who stand to gain kudos and funding."[6]

However it is that commercial interests contribute to the causes of childhood obesity or to our perception of it, the salience of the issue remains the same. As Dawes puts it: "Childhood obesity in America touches on important values and facets of American life—the nature of childhood, parents' responsibilities, economic and political duties, family values, pediatric medicine, economics and consumption, and the nature of progress and scientific achievement."[7]

The authors in *At Issue: Childhood Obesity* present a wide range of viewpoints concerning the causes, consequences, and efforts to combat America's childhood obesity epidemic.

6. Laura Dawes, *Childhood Obesity in America*. Cambridge, MA: Harvard University Press, 2014, p. 10.
7. Ibid.

1

Childhood Obesity Is an Urgent Public Health Problem

White House Task Force on Childhood Obesity

President Barack Obama created the White House Task Force on Childhood Obesity in 2010, charging it with reducing childhood obesity in the United States. The task force is designed to support First Lady Michelle Obama's "Let's Move!" campaign to promote healthy eating habits and physical activity.

With one in every three American children being overweight or obese, childhood obesity has become a national health crisis. Obesity seriously affects children's health, increases health-care costs, and even compromises the country's military readiness because young people are too out of shape to serve. By learning more about how and why children become obese, public health officials hope to create better community initiatives to combat childhood obesity. Among the key strategies they have identified are getting children to be more physically active and ensuring they have access to healthy foods, both at school and in their communities.

The childhood obesity epidemic in America is a national health crisis. One in every three children (31.7%) ages 2–19 is overweight or obese. The life-threatening consequences of this epidemic create a compelling and critical call for action that cannot be ignored. Obesity is estimated to cause 112,000 deaths per year in the United States, and one-third of all chil-

White House Task Force on Childhood Obesity, "The Challenge We Face," in *Solving the Problem of Childhood Obesity Within a Generation*. Washington, DC: US Government Printing Office, 2010. All rights reserved. Reproduced with permission.

dren born in the year 2000 are expected to develop diabetes during their lifetime. The current generation may even be on track to have a shorter lifespan than their parents.

There is considerable knowledge about the risk factors associated with childhood obesity.

Along with the effects on our children's health, childhood obesity imposes substantial economic costs. Each year, obese adults incur an estimated $1,429 more in medical expenses than their normal-weight peers. Overall, medical spending on adults that was attributed to obesity topped approximately $40 billion in 1998, and by 2008, increased to an estimated $147 billion. Excess weight is also costly during childhood, estimated at $3 billion per year in direct medical costs.

Childhood obesity also creates potential implications for military readiness. More than one quarter of all Americans ages 17–24 are unqualified for military service because they are too heavy. As one military leader noted recently, "We have an obesity crisis in the country. There's no question about it. These are the same young people we depend on to serve in times of need and ultimately protect this nation."

While these statistics are striking, there is much reason to be hopeful. There is considerable knowledge about the risk factors associated with childhood obesity. Research and scientific information on the causes and consequences of childhood obesity form the platform on which to build our national policies and partner with the private sector to end the childhood obesity epidemic. Effective policies and tools to guide healthy eating and active living are within our grasp. This report will focus and expand on what we can do together to:

1. create a healthy start on life for our children, from pregnancy through early childhood;

2. empower parents and caregivers to make healthy choices for their families;

3. serve healthier food in schools;

4. ensure access to healthy, affordable food; and

5. increase opportunities for physical activity.

What Is Obesity?

Obesity is defined as excess body fat. Because body fat is difficult to measure directly, obesity is often measured by body mass index (BMI), a common scientific way to screen for whether a person is underweight, normal weight, overweight, or obese. BMI adjusts weight for height, and while it is not a perfect indicator of obesity, it is a valuable tool for public health.

Adults with a BMI between 25.0 and 29.9 are considered overweight, those with a BMI of 30 or more are considered obese, and those with a BMI of 40 or more are considered extremely obese. For children and adolescents, these BMI categories are further divided by sex and age because of the changes that occur during growth and development. Growth charts from the Centers for Disease Control and Prevention (CDC) are used to calculate children's BMI. Children and adolescents with a BMI between the 85th and 94th percentiles are generally considered overweight, and those with a BMI at or above the sex-and age-specific 95th percentile of population on this growth chart are typically considered obese.

Childhood obesity is more common among certain racial and ethnic groups than others.

Determining what is a healthy weight for children is challenging, even with precise measures. BMI is often used as a screening tool, since a BMI in the overweight or obese range often, but not always, indicates that a child is at increased risk for health problems. A clinical assessment and other indicators must also be considered when evaluating a child's overall health and development.

Who Does Obesity Impact? Prevalence and Trends

By gaining a deeper understanding of individuals who are impacted by obesity, we can better shape policies to combat it. Since 1980, obesity has become dramatically more common among Americans of all ages. Prevalence estimates of obesity in the U.S. are derived from the National Health and Nutrition Examination Survey (NHANES), conducted by the National Center for Health Statistics of the CDC. Between the survey periods 1976–80 and 2007–08, obesity has more than doubled among adults (rising from 15% to 34%), and more than tripled among children and adolescents (rising from 5% to 17%).

The rapid increase in childhood obesity in the 1980s and 1990s has slowed, with no significant increase in recent years. However, among boys ages 6–19, very high BMI (at or above the 97th percentile) became more common between 1999–2000 and 2007–08; about 15% of boys in this age group are in this category.

Childhood obesity is more common among certain racial and ethnic groups than others. Obesity rates are highest among non-Hispanic black girls and Hispanic boys. Obesity is particularly common among American Indian/Native Alaskan children. A study of four year-olds found that obesity was more than two times more common among American Indian/Native Alaskan children (31%) than among white (16%) or Asian (13%) children. This rate was higher than any other racial or ethnic group studied.

Among adults, obesity rates are sometimes associated with lower incomes, particularly among women. Women with higher incomes tend to have lower BMI, and the opposite is true, those with higher BMI have lower incomes. A study in the early 2000s found that about 38% of non-Hispanic white women who qualified for the Supplemental Nutrition Assistance Program (known then as food stamps), were obese, and about 26% of those above 350% of the poverty line were obese. Also, a recent study of American adults found lower rates of obesity among individuals with more education. Specifically, the study found that nearly 35% of adults with less than a high school degree were obese, compared to 21% of those with a bachelor's degree or higher.

The relationship between income and obesity in children is less consistent than among adult women, and sometimes even points in the opposite direction. Another study from the early 2000s found that only among white girls were higher incomes associated with lower BMI. Among African-American girls, the prevalence of obesity actually increased with higher socioeconomic status, suggesting that efforts to reduce ethnic disparities in obesity must target factors other than income and education, such as environmental, social, and cultural factors.

Obesity is the most significant risk factor for type 2 diabetes.

Across the country, the prevalence of obesity has been found to be highest in southeast states such as Alabama, Mississippi, South Carolina, Tennessee, and West Virginia, as well as in Oklahoma. It is lowest in Colorado. Another study showed obesity was most common among adults in the Midwest and the South, as well as among adults who did not live in metropolitan areas.

How Does Obesity Impact Our Health?

Obese adults have an increased risk for many diseases, including type 2 diabetes, heart disease, some forms of arthritis, and several cancers. Overweight and obese children are more likely to become obese adults. Specifically, one study found that obese 6–8 year-olds were approximately ten times more likely to become obese adults than those with lower BMIs. The association may be stronger for obese adolescents than younger children. Obese children are also more likely to have increased risk of heart disease. One study found that approximately 70% of obese children had high levels (greater than 90th percentile) of at least one key risk factor for heart disease, and approximately 30% had high levels of at least two risk factors. There is evidence that heart disease develops in early childhood and is exacerbated by obesity, and people as young as 21 have been found to display early physical signs of heart disease due to obesity. Obese children are also more likely to develop asthma.

Obesity is the most significant risk factor for type 2 diabetes, a disease once called "adult onset diabetes" because it occurred almost exclusively in adults until childhood obesity started to rise substantially. The number of hospitalizations for type 2 diabetes among Americans in their 20s has gone up substantially, for example. A 2001 study found that more than 75% of children ages 10 and over with type 2 diabetes were obese. Type 2 diabetes occurs more frequently among some racial and ethnic minority groups, and rates among American Indians are particularly high.

In addition to the physical health consequences, severely obese children report a lower health-related quality of life (a measure of their physical, emotional, educational, and social well-being). In fact, one study found that they have a similar quality of life as children diagnosed with cancer. Childhood obesity is a highly stigmatized condition, often associated with low self-esteem, and obese children are more likely than nonobese children to feel sad, lonely, and nervous. Obesity during childhood is also associated with some psychiatric disorders, including depression and binge-eating disorder, which may both contribute to and be adversely impacted by obesity.

What Causes Obesity?

A child's risk of becoming obese may even begin before birth. Pregnant women who use tobacco, gain excessive weight, or have diabetes give birth to children who have an increased risk of being obese during their preschool years. Furthermore, although the evidence is not conclusive, rapid weight gain in early infancy has been shown to predict obesity later in life. Racial and ethnic differences in obesity may also be partly explained by differences in risk factors during the prenatal period and early life.

Among children, watching television or time spent on computers or gaming systems takes away from engaging in physical activity like organized sports or informal playing.

Studies show that early influences can affect obesity rates. The increased occurrence of obesity among children of obese parents suggests a genetic component. Multiple twin and adoption studies also indicate a strong genetic component to obesity. However, genes associated with obesity were present in the population prior to the current epidemic; genes only account for susceptibility to obesity and generally contribute to obesity only when other influences are at work. Genetic susceptibility to obesity is significantly shaped by the environment. In addition to genetic factors, recent research has focused on other factors, such as maternal nutrition, environmental toxins, and the prenatal environment, which may shape later risk for childhood obesity.

Environmental Factors During Childhood

There have been major changes in Americans' lifestyles over the last 30 years, as childhood obesity rates have been rising. This includes what and where we eat. Given the pace of modern life, Americans now consume more fast-food and sugar-sweetened beverages, eat outside the home more frequently, and spend less time enjoying family meals. In addition, prepared and processed food is easily accessible and inexpensive. These items are also heavily promoted, as evidenced in a Federal Trade Commission (FTC) report revealing that at least $1.6 billion is spent annually on food advertising directed to children and adolescents. All this adds up to poor eating habits. For example, 13% of the daily caloric intake for 12–19 year-olds now comes from sugar-sweetened beverages.

At the same time, adults and children alike are getting less physical activity. Some schools have cut back on activities like physical education and recess, in part due to budget pressures at the state and local level. And children are increasingly driven to school by car or bus, rather than walking or biking. In part, these shifts in transportation reflect changes in community design. Physical activity is higher in more "connected" communities that provide safe and reliable access to public transportation, as well as other forms of active transport like biking and walking.

Meanwhile, "screen time" has increased, including television viewing, which is directly associated with childhood and adult obesity. Among children, watching television or time spent on computers or gaming systems takes away from engaging in physical activity like organized sports or informal playing. It also has a more harmful effect on healthy eating habits; as children watch television, they are more likely to snack, including on the foods advertised. In addition, screen time has been associated with children getting less and poorer quality sleep, and insufficient sleep has been linked to a heightened risk of obesity.

What Can We Do?

While additional studies to identify the precise causes of obesity will be useful, we do not need to wait to identify specific actions that we can take as a society to prevent obesity. There are many examples of effective therapies for diseases whose cause has not been fully identified. For example, remission rates of acute lymphocytic leukemia in children have been dramatically improved over the last 20 years, although the causes of the disease remain uncertain.

Reducing childhood obesity does not have to be a costly endeavor. . . . [A] great deal can be accomplished without significant expenditures.

No single action alone will reverse the childhood obesity epidemic, although there is no question that improving eating habits and increasing physical activity are two critical strategies. As with tobacco prevention and control, comprehensive, multi-sectoral approaches are needed to address the many behavioral risk factors associated with obesity. These risk factors fall into three general categories: (1) material incentives, such as the cost of food or the desire to avoid poor health; (2) social norms, such as the nutritional and physical activity habits of friends and family, which influence us greatly; and (3) the broader environment, such as whether grocery stores and playgrounds are nearby or far away. Changes in each of these risk factors are possible. For example, with sound information, parents and caregivers will be able to seek out the most nutritious foods to improve their children's health; changes in social norms can be brought about through movements such as the successful seatbelt buckling campaigns of the late 20th century; and changes can be made in the broader environment by eliminating "food deserts" or "playground deserts."

In many parts of the country, we already have a head start, and initiatives that are already underway will provide instructive lessons. Comprehensive, community-wide efforts to reduce obesity have recently been initiated by both the public and private sectors. The American Recovery and Reinvestment Act of 2009 included $1 billion in funding for prevention and wellness investments, more than half of which was directed to prevention strategies to reduce tobacco use and obesity rates. Specifically, $373 million supported direct community-based interventions and $120 million supported state-based efforts in all 50 states and 25 communities in urban, rural, and tribal areas. Funds to support comprehensive strategies were awarded to states in February and to communities in March. The recently-enacted Patient Protection and Affordable Care Act, as amended by the Health Care and Education Affordability Reconciliation Act (collectively referred to as the "Affordable Care Act") provides for additional investments in chronic disease and improving public health, which could include community-based prevention strategies. In addition, the philanthropic sector has been leading the way with stepped-up, focused investments. For example, the Robert Wood Johnson Foundation has created a "Healthy Kids, Healthy Communities" initiative that is funding 50 communities to implement strategies to prevent childhood obesity, and the California Endowment recently launched a large-scale "Building Healthy Communities" project in 14 communities that will include a focus on childhood obesity prevention.

Our goal is to solve the problem of childhood obesity in a generation. Achieving that goal will mean returning to the expected levels in the population, before this epidemic began.

The Path Forward

Reducing childhood obesity does not have to be a costly endeavor, however. And indeed, in many communities it simply cannot be. Times are tough, and federal, state, local, and family budgets are all feeling squeezed. But a great deal can be accomplished without significant expenditures, and some steps may ultimately save money. While many of the recommendations in this report will require additional public resources, creative strategies can also be used to redirect resources or make more effective use of existing investments.

In total, this report presents a series of 70 specific recommendations, many of which can be implemented right away. Summarizing them broadly, they include:

- *Getting children a healthy start on life*, with good prenatal care for their parents; support for breastfeeding; adherence to limits on "screen time"; and quality child care settings with nutritious food and ample opportunity for young children to be physically active.

- *Empowering parents and caregivers* with simpler, more actionable messages about nutritional choices based on the latest *Dietary Guidelines for Americans*; improved labels on food and menus that provide clear information to help make healthy choices for children; reduced marketing of unhealthy products to children; and improved health care services, including BMI measurement for all children.

- *Providing healthy food in schools*, through improvements in federally-supported school lunches and breakfasts; upgrading the nutritional quality of other foods sold in schools; and improving nutrition education and the overall school environment.

- *Improving access to healthy, affordable food*, by eliminating "food deserts" in urban and rural America; lowering the relative prices of healthier foods; developing or reformulating food products to be healthier; and reducing the incidence of hunger, which has been linked to obesity.

- *Getting children more physically active*, through quality physical education, recess, and other opportunities in and after school; addressing aspects of the "built environment" that make it difficult for children to walk or bike safely in their communities; and improving access to safe parks, playgrounds, and indoor and outdoor recreational facilities.

Many of these recommendations are for activities to be undertaken by federal agencies. All such activities are subject to budgetary constraints, including the weighing of priorities and available resources by the Administration in formulating its annual budget and by Congress in legislating appropriations.

How Will We Know We Have Succeeded?

Our goal is to solve the problem of childhood obesity in a generation. Achieving that goal will mean returning to the expected levels in the population, before this epidemic began. That means *returning to a childhood obesity rate of just 5% by 2030*. Achieving this goal will require "bending the curve" fairly quickly, so that by 2015, there will be a 2.5% reduction in each of the current rates of overweight and obese children, and by 2020, a 5% reduction. Our progress can be charted through the CDC's annual National Health and Nutrition Examination Survey (NHANES), which is aggregated every two years.

In addition to monitoring the overall trends in childhood obesity, two key indicators will show the progress achieved:

1. *The number of children eating a healthy diet*, measured by those who follow the most recent, science-based *Dietary Guidelines for Americans (Dietary Guidelines)*. We can monitor our progress through the U.S. Department of Agriculture's (USDA) Healthy Eating Index (HEI), which reflects the intake of 12 dietary components: total fruit (including juice); whole fruit (not juice); total vegetables; dark green and orange vegetables and legumes; total grains; whole grains; milk products; meat and beans; oils; saturated fat; sodium; and calories from solid fats and added sugars. USDA generally regards a

score of at least 80 out of 100 points as reflecting a healthy diet. Currently, the average child scores a 55.9 on the HEI. To achieve a score of 80 for the average child by 2030, the average child should score 65 by 2015, and 70 by 2020. Two indicators should be monitored particularly closely:

- *Less added sugar in children's diets.* Children today consume a substantial amount of added sugars through a whole range of products. Using existing data sources, CDC's National Center for Health Statistics can determine how much added sugar children are currently consuming. Targets for reducing added sugar will then need to be established that track the overall goal of driving obesity rates down to 5% by 2030.

- *More fruits and vegetables.* Currently, children and adolescents consume far lower quantities of fruits and vegetables than recommended in the *Dietary Guidelines.* On average, children consumed only 64% of the recommended level of fruit and 46% of the recommended level of vegetables in 2003–04. Average fruit consumption should increase to 75% of the recommended level by 2015, 85% by 2020, and 100% by 2030; vegetable consumption should increase to 60% of recommended levels by 2015, 75% by 2020, and 100% by 2030.

2. *The number of children meeting current physical activity guidelines.* Right now, the only regular survey that shows whether children are meeting the Physical Activity Guidelines is limited to high school students, and regular data on younger children is not available. Resources will have to be redirected to develop a survey instrument that can provide a full picture of physical activity levels among children of all ages. Once baseline data is

available, targets for improving the level of physical activity among children will need to be established that track the overall goal of driving obesity rates down to 5% by 2030.

Additional benchmarks of success, tied to specific recommendations in this report, are included throughout. The Healthy People goals set every decade by experts convened by the U.S. Department of Health and Human Services will provide additional, complementary opportunities to measure our progress in helping children achieve and maintain a healthy weight.

Monitoring our progress and the impact of our interventions, so that we know what is working and what strategies or tactics need to be adjusted, will be critically important. This is not an easy challenge, but it is one that we can solve as a society, and within a generation.

2

It Is Not the Government's Job to Fight Childhood Obesity

Daren Bakst

Daren Bakst studies and writes about agriculture subsidies, property rights, environmental policy, food labeling, and related issues at The Heritage Foundation, a conservative think tank based in Washington, DC.

First Lady Michelle Obama's campaign against childhood obesity is an unwelcome government intrusion into how parents choose to raise their children. The "Healthy, Hunger-Free Kids Act" is a misguided effort to police what American children eat. The program will ultimately prove to be a failure because schools are incurring massive costs to comply with it, while many children won't eat the food and plate waste is skyrocketing. The federal government should not be in the business of mandating menus, and local school districts and communities should have more say on the issue. It is not the government's job to act as a parent.

[First Lady] Michelle Obama thinks she knows what your children should eat. She's adamant about promoting her nutrition policies for kids, even the new and disastrous school meal standards implementing the "Healthy, Hunger-Free Kids Act."

In a recent MSN interview, Michelle Obama revealed her own struggles with getting her kids to eat properly before she

Daren Bakst, "The First Parent of The United States," heritage.org, June 30, 2014. Copyright © 2014 Heritage Foundation. All rights reserved. Reproduced with permission.

came to the White House. This apparently led to a major realization: "I thought to myself, if a Princeton- and Harvard-educated professional woman doesn't know how to adequately feed her kids, then what are other parents going through who don't have access to the information I have?"

This motivated her to take on childhood obesity. She set her sights on schools because "the most important place to start tackling this issue is in our schools."

Schools are incurring massive costs to comply with the standards. Some schools have reportedly transferred money out of their teaching budgets to cover the food costs.

But attending Ivy-League schools doesn't magically make someone better parent material than an individual who attended a public university, or, dare it be said, someone who didn't attend college. It also doesn't mean that she should be a co-parent to your children. Make no mistake; the underlying assumption is that federal technocrats and educated individuals such as her need to act on your behalf to meet the best interests of your children.

This arrogance is on display in the current controversy over the new and restrictive federal school meal standards. Since the 2010–11 school year, participation in the school lunch program has fallen dramatically after more than a decade of growth. Most of the decline occurred in the 2012–2013 school year, when participation fell by over a million students. This just so happens to be the first year that the standards were in effect.

High Costs for Compliance

Schools are incurring massive costs to comply with the standards. Some schools have reportedly transferred money out of their teaching budgets to cover the food costs. There's massive plate waste, food storage and equipment costs, and little flexibility for local schools to meet the needs of their students.

Michelle Obama has scolded anyone who dares to address concerns about these standards, including the School Nutrition Association (SNA), which represents more than 55,000 school nutrition professionals. That may be the only way to counter the legitimate concerns that the school system's foot soldiers are seeing firsthand.

SNA, though, isn't the only organization highlighting the problems. The independent Government Accountability Office did a survey of school nutrition officers. These officials expressed similar concerns, including problems with plate waste and food costs.

According to the National School Board Association, "School boards cannot ignore the higher costs and operational issues created by the rigid mandates of the Healthy, Hunger-Free Kids Act."

As the self-appointed First Parent of the United States, Michelle Obama is effectively making that infamous parental argument, "Because I said so." She just ignores all the problems that have been identified. The big argument that she makes along with her allies is 90 percent of schools are meeting the standards.

This is an irrelevant point. It doesn't address the problems that have been identified, such as plate waste, food costs, participation, or whether long-term compliance is feasible. In fact, significant compliance should have been expected; otherwise, schools wouldn't be so concerned about the massive burden they currently face by having to comply with the standards.

More Flexibility Is Needed

These standards should be changed to create more power and flexibility for parents and local school officials. In the meantime, the "radical" idea in the House agriculture appropriations bill of giving one-year compliance waivers to financially struggling schools should be adopted. A waiver doesn't weaken the standards in any way; it doesn't touch them.

This entire issue, though, is really about the proper role of the federal government. While Michelle Obama is pushing for rigid federal control of school meals, the alternative is respecting parents who know their children's needs better than anyone else, even better than Michelle Obama. The alternative also includes respecting local school officials, who know their communities better than the federal government.

If parents don't like meal standards, they can and will complain directly and in person to local officials. Parents don't have the same recourse with faceless and nameless bureaucrats in Washington, D.C.

It's a bit strange that Michelle Obama, who admits she had problems feeding her own children, is now taking the lead to aggressively push what other people's kids should eat. Even though she acknowledges she hasn't been infallible when it comes to child nutrition, she can't admit that these new and controversial national standards might be problematic. A good parent knows when to let go.

3

Childhood Obesity Fuels High Health-Care Costs

Ross A. Hammond

Ross A. Hammond is a senior fellow in economic studies at the Brookings Institution, where he is director of the Center on Social Dynamics and Policy.

The obesity epidemic—and childhood obesity in particular—has far-reaching implications for the American health-care system. The health risks associated with being obese, such as heart disease, diabetes, high blood pressure, high cholesterol, and asthma, translate to significantly higher medical costs for obese individuals. Childhood obesity alone is estimated to cause $14.1 billion in medical costs each year, and by some estimates nearly 21 percent of all health-care spending is currently obesity related. As today's obese children become tomorrow's obese adults that number is likely to grow and become an "unsustainable burden" on the health-care system.

[I]n her 2012 paper, "Curing Health Care," Brookings Institution senior fellow] Alice Rivlin highlights the twin health care challenges facing America and the next president: covering the uninsured while curbing unsustainable increases in health care costs and their impact on the debt. She provides a compelling argument for how to address these challenges through health care legislation. I would like to focus here on the role that investment in *public health* and *prevention* can play as a complementary strategy for controlling health care spending.

Perhaps the most pressing public health challenge for the United States today is the epidemic of overweight and obesity, which is linked to an array of costly and debilitating health consequences. According to data from the National Center for Health Statistics, two in three American adults are now overweight, including one in three who are obese. A recent study also found that almost one-third of children and adolescents are overweight or obese. These rates are even higher among ethnic minorities, rural populations, and those with low income or education. The health risks associated with obesity reported by the Institute of Medicine include a much higher incidence of cardiovascular disease, diabetes, several cancers, hypertension, high cholesterol, asthma, osteoarthritis, and liver disease.

Keeping the costs of obesity from overwhelming the health care system will require a renewed focus by the next president on obesity prevention.

Obesity in Health-Care Dollars

Not surprisingly, then, the obesity epidemic is a major driver of health care costs in the United States, and the costs may continue to increase significantly in the future if it is not controlled. The increased health risks for major disease that come with obesity carry not only a high social price tag but also a high economic one—relative medical costs for the obese are estimated to be 36 to 100 percent higher than for Americans of healthy weight. A 2009 study found that childhood obesity alone is responsible for $14.1 billion in direct medical costs annually. By some estimates, *nearly 21 percent of all current medical spending* in the United States is now obesity related. A significant proportion of these medical costs is paid by Medicaid and Medicare, and one recent analysis concluded that total Medicaid spending would be almost 12 percent lower in the absence of obesity. Beyond direct medical spending, additional costs from obesity are driven by increased rates of disability and by reduced productivity.

The impact of obesity on health care spending is likely to increase in the coming years unless further preventative steps are taken. Although recent data suggest that obesity rates may now be leveling off after a period of very rapid growth, the epidemic in children is especially worrisome because most obese children become obese adults. Childhood obesity means more chronic disease will begin earlier in life for more people—driving up lifetime costs considerably. For example, type 2 diabetes (for which obesity is a particularly strong risk factor) occurred primarily in adults until recently, but the Centers for Disease Control report that it is now beginning in childhood for more Americans. A recent report in the *Journal of the American Medical Association* estimates that one-third of all children born in the United States today (and one-half of all Latino and African American children) will develop type 2 diabetes in their lifetime. Even if the epidemic does not worsen, these costs are likely to prove an unsustainable burden on the health system given the long-term growth of the federal debt.

Prevention Can Bring Savings

Keeping the costs of obesity from overwhelming the health care system will require a renewed focus by the next president on *obesity prevention*. This has the potential to contain costs much more effectively than the mere treatment of obesity-related chronic health conditions. Early childhood can be an especially important period—once obesity develops, a powerful set of physiological processes and behavior patterns make it challenging to reverse. From the perspective of health care costs, early prevention can produce substantial savings. According to an analysis in the *American Journal of Public Health*, as little as a 5 percent reduction in the prevalence of diabetes and hypertension would save almost $25 billion annually in medium-term health care costs.

Prevention is important, but designing effective prevention efforts remains challenging. The drivers of the obesity epidemic are complex and multifaceted, so there is likely no single solution. Continued investment in research on effective prevention strategies is needed, especially in support of what the Institute of Medicine and National Institutes of Health refer to as new "systems" approaches. Indeed, it may be critical to *coordinate* policy across many domains and levels of scale in order to see a rapid change in the obesity epidemic. To be most effective, prevention efforts must focus not just on educating individuals or on changing environments, but on doing *both* together.

The Next President's Role

The next president should take several steps to address the major public health challenge of obesity and help avoid the unsustainable health care costs it will generate:

- Renew the emphasis on prevention efforts. Prevention is especially important, given the role of childhood influences in the development of overweight and the challenge of reversing obesity once entrenched.

- Increase investment in public health research to develop an evidence base that supports the design and testing of powerful new prevention strategies for the future. As the scientific community emphasizes, innovative approaches are greatly needed to continue to improve how policy addresses the complex drivers of obesity.

- Coordinate public policy across domains and agencies. Many policy areas "outside" of health—including education, housing, transportation, agriculture, and tax policy—have strong effects on public health and obesity. A more systemic approach that takes into account connections across these areas should be a central element in an effective obesity prevention strategy.

4

Public Agrees on Obesity's Impact, Not Government's Role

Pew Research Center

The Pew Research Center is a nonpartisan think tank based in Washington, DC. It conducts public opinion polling, demographic research, media analysis, and other social science research.

According to a recent survey by the Pew Research Center, most Americans view obesity as a very serious health problem. However, even though six in ten people believe government programs could do "a lot" or "some" to reduce obesity, more than half say the government should not play a significant role in trying to do so. And while two-thirds support laws that require calorie counts to be listed on menus, a similar majority opposes limiting the size of sugary drinks; more than half support a ban on advertising unhealthy food during children's programming and a similar majority opposes raising taxes on sodas and junk food. The American public remains divided on the issue of the government's role in reducing obesity.

Most Americans (69%) see obesity as a very serious public health problem, substantially more than the percentages viewing alcohol abuse, cigarette smoking and AIDS in the same terms. In addition, a broad majority believes that obesity is not just a problem that affects individuals: 63% say obesity has consequences for society beyond the personal impact on individuals. Just 31% say it impacts the individuals who are obese but not society more broadly.

Yet, the public has mixed opinions about what, if anything, the government should do about the issue. A 54% majority does not want the government to play a significant role in reducing obesity, while 42% say the government should play a significant role. And while some proposals for reducing obesity draw broad support, others are decidedly unpopular.

About seven-in-ten adults say [obesity] is an extremely (24%) or very (45%) serious public health problem.

The new national survey by the Pew Research Center, conducted Oct. 30–Nov. 6 among 2,003 adults, finds that two-thirds (67%) favor requiring chain restaurants to list calorie counts on menus. But just 31% support limits on the size of sugary soft drinks in restaurants and convenience stores— 67% oppose this idea. More than half (55%) favor banning TV ads of unhealthy foods during children's programming, but barely a third (35%) supports raising taxes on sugary soft drinks and unhealthy foods. On each of these policies, Democrats and women are more supportive than Republicans, independents and men. (The survey was conducted before the Food and Drug Administration's proposal last Thursday to severely restrict trans fats nationwide.)

While most agree that obesity is a very serious public health problem, the public is divided as to whether the country is making progress or losing ground in dealing with obesity. Slightly more people say the U.S. is losing ground (34%) than making progress (28%), with 36% saying things are about the same as they have been.

How much can the government do to reduce obesity? Roughly six-in-ten believe government policies and programs can do "a lot" (26%) or "some" (35%); about one-in-five

(22%) say that government policies can do "not much" and 14% say they can do "nothing at all" to reduce obesity.

The Scope of the Problem

Obesity ranks high among perceived public health problems: About seven-in-ten adults say it is an extremely (24%) or very (45%) serious public health problem. Americans view obesity as a less serious public health problem than cancer (79%), but similar to mental illness (67%) and more than abuse of prescription drugs (63%) or alcohol (54%).

Far fewer Americans say the nation is making progress in dealing with obesity (28%) than in dealing with cancer (54% making progress), AIDS (48%) or cigarette smoking (45%). But more say progress is being made on obesity than on mental illness (19%), alcohol abuse (17%) or prescription drug abuse (16%).

Those who see obesity as a very serious problem are about twice as likely as those who do not to say the nation is losing ground in dealing with the issue (40% vs. 19%).

Women are slightly more likely than men to say that obesity is a serious public health problem (72% vs. 66%). But women also are more likely to believe that the country has been making progress on the issue (32% vs. 24% of men).

About six-in-ten Americans (63%) say obesity has consequences for society that go beyond personal impact.

In addition, Hispanics (83%) and blacks (75%) are more likely than whites (65%) to rate obesity as a serious public health problem. Blacks are more optimistic on the issue: 37% believe the country is making progress on obesity while just 16% say we are losing ground. By comparison, 39% of Hispanics and 36% of whites feel we are losing ground.

More Democrats (77%) than Republicans (61%) view obesity as a very serious public health problem. Democrats are more likely than Republicans to see the country as making progress (36% vs. 24%).

Those who describe themselves as overweight are as likely as others to say that obesity is a very serious public health problem (70% vs. 69%) and have similar views about whether the country is making progress or losing ground on the issue.

More than Just an Individual Problem

About six-in-ten Americans (63%) say obesity has consequences for society that go beyond personal impact. Only about half as many (31%) say obesity does not have a major societal impact beyond the individual level. Majorities in virtually every demographic and political subgroup say obesity has social consequences beyond the individuals affected.

Republicans (60%), Democrats (67%) and independents (63%) are about equally likely to say obesity has social consequences, as are men (62%) and women (64%). Perhaps the biggest divide is by education: 76% of college graduates say obesity has social consequences beyond the individuals affected, compared with 68% of those with some college and 51% of those with a high school degree or less.

Among those younger than 30, 55% say obesity has consequences for society beyond the personal impacts, 39% say it does not have a major societal impact. Among older age groups, about three-in-ten say obesity does not have a major impact on society.

Limited Support for Government
Role in Reducing Obesity

While most see obesity as a substantial public health issue, there is limited support for the government playing a major role in anti-obesity efforts. Overall, 42% say government should play a significant role in reducing obesity, 54% say it should not.

While majorities of Republicans and Democrats say obesity has broad social consequences, there are sharp partisan differences about whether the government should have a role in reducing obesity. By a margin of 60%–37%, Democrats believe the government should play a significant role in curbing obesity. But just 20% of Republicans say this, while 77% of Republicans do not want the government to play a significant role. Among independents, more say the government should not play a significant role (56%) than say that it should (41%).

There are differences within the Republican Party on this issue. Nearly nine-in-ten (89%) Republicans and Republican leaners who agree with the Tea Party oppose a significant role for the government in reducing obesity. Among non-Tea Party Republicans, 65% oppose a government role.

Not surprisingly, views on what government *should* do are closely linked to perceptions of what the government *can* do. About one-in-four adults (26%) think government policies can do "a lot" to reduce obesity and 35% say it can do "some." Roughly one-in-five (22%) say that government policies can do "not much" and 14% say they can do "nothing at all" to reduce obesity.

About half (54%) of adults ages 18–29 say the government should play a significant role in reducing obesity, compared with just 33% of those ages 65 and older.

Among those who think that government policies and programs can do a lot to reduce obesity, 84% want the government to play a significant role. Nearly the opposite is true of those who believe such policies can do not much or nothing at all—83% think the government should not play a significant role. Those who think government policies can do some to reduce obesity are split: 47% think the government should play a significant role and 51% say it should not.

Among the public overall, majorities of blacks (66%) and Hispanics (69%) say that government should play a significant role in reducing obesity. By contrast, whites are far less likely to think the government should be involved. Just a third of whites (33%) say the government should play a significant role in addressing obesity, while 64% disagree.

There also are age differences in views of the government's role on obesity. About half (54%) of adults ages 18–29 say the government should play a significant role in reducing obesity, compared with just 33% of those ages 65 and older.

While college graduates are more likely than those who have not attended college to describe obesity as having societal consequences, they are no more likely to support major government efforts to deal with the issue or to believe that government anti-obesity efforts are likely to be effective.

People who describe themselves as overweight are about as likely to want a significant government role (40%) as those who describe themselves as about right or underweight (43%).

Demographic Divides on Specific Food Policies

When it comes to specific public policies aimed at reducing obesity, the public is of two minds. Proposals focused on information and advertising draw more support than opposition. But proposals that would affect an individual's choice more directly are broadly opposed.

Most people are in favor of requiring chain restaurants to list calorie counts on menus (67%) and most also support a ban on advertising unhealthy food during children's television programming (55%). But majorities oppose a limit on soda size in restaurants and convenience stores (67%) as well as higher taxes on unhealthy foods and soft drinks (64%).

In recent years, New York City and other cities have banned artificial trans fats from restaurants, a policy that slightly more Americans would oppose (52%) than favor

(44%). Last Thursday—after the survey was completed—the FDA proposed banning the cholesterol-laden trans fats because they are not "generally recognized as safe."

All five of the policies have more support from women than men, by about 10 percentage points in each case. And in all five cases, Democrats favor a more restrictive food policy than Republicans and independents.

Among Republicans, only calorie counts in chain restaurants receive majority support (59% favor). (A provision of the Affordable Care Act, requiring restaurants with 20 or more locations to post calorie counts, is currently in the process of being implemented.)

More Democrats (63%) than Republicans (47%) favor banning ads for unhealthy food on children's TV shows.

Limiting the size of soft drinks in restaurants and convenience stores—a policy passed in New York City earlier this year, but invalidated by a New York judge—faces broad opposition across virtually all groups. Democrats oppose this idea by a 57% to 41% margin. Opposition outpaces support among independents by 69% to 30%, and just 19% of Republicans would favor soda-size limits while 78% would oppose them.

There also are partisan differences in opinions about raising taxes on sugary soft drinks and unhealthy foods: 45% of Democrats, 33% of independents and just 24% of Republicans favor higher taxes on unhealthy foods. Among Democrats, a majority of liberals (67%) supports this proposal compared with 38% of the party's conservatives and moderates.

More Democrats (63%) than Republicans (47%) favor banning ads for unhealthy food on children's TV shows, and while there is less support overall for banning restaurant trans fats, the partisan gap in views is similar (51% of Democrats favor vs. 35% of Republicans).

Nearly half of those under 30 favor raising taxes on sugary soft drinks and unhealthy food (48%) and 45% favor limiting the size of sugary soft drinks. By contrast, only about a quarter of those 50 and older support each of these proposals.

More non-whites (43%) than whites (31%) support raising taxes on unhealthy foods. Similarly, 43% of non-whites and only 25% of whites support limiting soda sizes. (The sample size for these questions was too small to allow for comparisons between blacks and Hispanics separately.)

About the Survey

The analysis in this report is based on telephone interviews conducted October 30–November 6, 2013 among a national sample of 2,003 adults, 18 years of age or older, living in all 50 U.S. states and the District of Columbia (1,001 respondents were interviewed on a landline telephone, and 1,002 were interviewed on a cell phone, including 524 who had no landline telephone). The survey was conducted by interviewers at Princeton Data Source under the direction of Princeton Survey Research Associates International. A combination of landline and cell phone random digit dial samples were used; both samples were provided by Survey Sampling International. Interviews were conducted in English and Spanish. Respondents in the landline sample were selected by randomly asking for the youngest adult male or female who is now at home. Interviews in the cell sample were conducted with the person who answered the phone, if that person was an adult 18 years of age or older. For detailed information about our survey methodology, see http://people-press.org/methodology/.

The combined landline and cell phone sample are weighted using an iterative technique that matches gender, age, education, race, Hispanic origin and nativity and region to parameters from the 2011 Census Bureau's American Community Survey and population density to parameter's from the Decennial Census. The sample also is weighted to match current patterns of telephone status and relative usage of landline and cell phones (for those with both), based on extrapolations from the 2012 National Health Interview Survey. The weighting procedure also accounts for the fact that respondents with both landline and cell phones have a greater probability of being included in the combined sample and adjusts for household size among respondents with a landline phone. Sampling errors and statistical tests of significance take into account the effect of weighting.

5

Fast Food Is a Major Cause of Childhood Obesity

Megan M. Kluge

Megan M. Kluge was a social science major at the University of Maryland University College when she wrote this viewpoint.

Childhood obesity is influenced by many factors, including familial eating patterns, media exposure, and children's television advertising, but one of the most complex is fast food. Research shows that children who are overweight are able to correctly identify more fast food brands than their normal-weight peers, and students who go to schools near fast food restaurants are heavier than those who go to schools that don't have fast food outlets nearby. While more research needs to be done on the link between fast food and childhood obesity, many experts are calling for public policies to limit the proximity of fast food outlets to schools.

Childhood obesity is a serious epidemic, affecting children across the world. In our country alone, 17% of all children and adolescents are now obese, triple the rate from just a generation ago. This drastic increase leads researchers and ordinary citizens alike to speculate about possible causes. Fast food consumption is one potential cause that has received widespread attention. Many researchers have looked at the relationship between fast food and childhood obesity from various angles. Some of these include the influence of family, the media, and the proximity of fast food restaurants to schools and homes. Examining the interrelationships of these angles can lead to a better understanding of the relationship between childhood obesity and fast food, and from this multi-angle viewpoint, we can see that no single aspect is solely to blame.

If a child grows up in a household with healthy parents and learns the value of making smart food choices, the child will likely continue these habits, as they get older.

Family Influence

There is no question that a child first learns eating habits in the home. But with parents being pulled in many directions and seemingly having an endless amount of responsibilities and obligations, fast food can often times be an appealing alternative to cooking at home. Fast food restaurants have many kid-friendly selections but the nutritional value of such meals is usually lacking. A study conducted by a group of researchers in Houston showed that just 3% of kids' meals offered at a variety of fast food restaurants met nutritional standards set forth by the National School Lunch Program. The same study showed that making a few small tweaks when ordering the meal could be the difference between a meal being considered healthy or unhealthy. For instance, a parent could order milk rather than soda or apple slices instead of fries. Condiments also make a difference; mayonnaise or oil can make the meal too fatty. A parent could order the meal without these condiments. By making these small adjustments, a parent can teach their children how to make healthy food choices and perhaps avoid becoming a statistic of childhood obesity.

Eating Fast Food at Home Rather than Away

Even in other countries the familial influence on a child's food choices and potential to become obese is strong. In a study conducted in Australia, researchers studied four key factors that they believe contribute to childhood obesity: the frequency of eating breakfast, eating while watching television, eating junk food at home, and eating fast food away from home. Researchers compiled the results based on these criteria and revisited most of the participating families three years later. What the researchers found in regard to the consumption of fast food is interesting. Eating fast food away from home was not necessarily associated with an increase in body mass index (BMI) rates at the time of follow-up. However, those who ate fast food at home were more likely to be overweight. The researchers speculate that the participants in the latter category might be watching television while eating, which can lead to overeating. The link between being overweight and consuming fast food at home does not take into consideration, however, the specific selections made in regard to fast food. As pointed out above by [the Houston] study, modifying fast food choices has the potential to make a difference.

[One research study] showed that those students who attended school near fast food restaurants were heavier than their counterparts who attended school not near a fast food restaurant.

Additional research points out that "family structures and patterns provide, in large part, the micro contexts within which meanings of food and eating practices are negotiated and developed". If a child grows up in a household with healthy parents and learns the value of making smart food choices, the child will likely continue these habits, as they get older. However, if a child is raised in a home with a pantry full of junk food and does not learn how to recognize food's nutritional value, the child will probably carry this with them into adulthood. The way a family consumes food is also an important factor; it is often suggested that eating at the table is best [and some research has] shown that eating in front of the television can potentially have a negative impact.

Media Influence

Even if a family practices healthy eating habits, the media will always find a way to influence children. Most fast food establishments offer kids' meals in bright, attractive packaging that often come with a toy. A result of such marketing is an increased recognizance of these brands by young children. In an attempt to understand and measure this recognizance, researchers conducted a study in a matching game-like fashion. [The researchers] were interested, in part, in recognition rates of fast food and other food products by young children as well as the type of food logo recognized by children and some characteristics about the children themselves. The game consisted of children matching the logo of restaurants with a type of food offered there. Children who had a higher BMI were able to correctly identify more fast food logos than children with lower BMI rates. The researchers in this study speculate that perhaps the marketing strategies used by these companies are successful in gaining the attention of children who, in turn, influence their parents' behavior when it comes to food purchasing. This is a clever way for fast food restaurants to ensure continued patronage by children and parents alike.

Children's Television Advertising

In addition to overt marketing strategies by fast food restaurants, children can also be the targeted audience of television commercials. Researchers conducted a study for the National Bureau of Economic Research [NBER] to determine if banning fast food ads during children's television programming would have any effect on the number of overweight or obese children. Through their study, researchers concluded that banning these ads would reduce the number of overweight children ages 3–11 by 18% and would reduce the number of overweight 12- to 18-year olds by 14%. The study also mentions that raising the price for fast food advertisements would be equally effective, as it would significantly reduce the number of ads on the air. However, banning television ads is not as easy as it seems, and the researchers note that the best way to ensure children are not viewing fast food ads on television is to limit the amount of television they are viewing as a whole. This point reiterates the parental responsibility brought forth [earlier]; parents are in a position to limit what their children are exposed to.

Does Proximity to Fast Food Matter?

Another important factor is the proximity of fast food restaurants in relation to schools and homes. Many studies have been done from this angle, and have uncovered an array of results. B. Davis and C. Carpenter conducted a popular study in 2009 in California. To calculate the proximity of fast food restaurants to schools, the researchers referred to a database of geo-coordinates from middle and high schools from the California Department of Education. They also utilized a database of restaurants in the state that included geo-coordinates. The third component of this calculation was a list of restaurant brands classified as being "top limited-service restaurants", or fast food restaurants. Using this formula, the researchers defined "near" as being (at least) one fast food restaurant within half a mile. Including these three components seems to be a very thorough calculation and a good way to determine the proximity. In regard to the student participants, the researchers relied on student responses to the 2002–2005 California Healthy Kids Survey (CHKS). It is an anonymous survey asking multiple questions about several topics related to health behaviors. Almost a third of the sample of students was overweight, and 12% was obese. The researchers' main finding showed that those students who attended school near fast food restaurants were heavier than their counterparts who attended school not near a fast food restaurant.

The topic of childhood obesity and its relationship to fast food is not just an issue in the United States.... [O]ther nations are also battling this issue.

Other studies yield different results. A study conducted by D. Crawford, et al. (2008) focused on the proximity of fast food restaurants to participants' homes rather than schools. This study defined and calculated proximity in a manner similar to Davis and Carpenter's method. The researchers defined "near" as being within 2km. In addition to including the BMI rates of child participants, the BMI of the children's parents was also incorporated. The results are quite different from the study conducted by Davis and Carpenter. "Among older boys and girls, those with at least one fast food outlet within 2km of their home had lower BMI [rates]". Equally intriguing were the results concerning the fathers in the study. "Among adult males, the further they lived from a fast food outlet, the higher their BMI". These results clearly do not support the notion that being in close proximity to fast food restaurants increases the risk of being overweight or obese.

Convenience Stores Boost Obesity

Other studies acknowledge that fast food restaurants located near schools can have negative effects, but also point out that fast food restaurants are not a child's only option for junk food after school. [One such study] sought to find associations between schools located near fast food restaurants, convenience stores, and supermarkets and the rates of overweight students in California. Their calculation of "proximity" is similar to that of [others], however, instead of merely defining "near" as being within a half a mile or within 2km, researchers in this study took into account actual pedestrian walking.

With this in mind, their definition of "near" was defined as within a 10-minute walk of the school. The results showed that there is indeed a positive correlation between the rates of overweight students and the presence of nearby convenience stores and fast food restaurants.

There are two interesting results in this study. First, the presence of supermarkets showed no relation with the rates of overweight students. This is surprising because supermarkets have the largest selection of food products compared to convenience stores or fast food restaurants. Second, convenience stores showed stronger correlations with rates of overweight students than fast food restaurants. These results show that fast food restaurants located within close proximity to schools or homes do not necessarily mean there will be an increase in rates of childhood obesity.

Childhood Obesity Around the World

The topic of childhood obesity and its relationship to fast food is not just an issue in the United States. As shown by the studies conducted in Australia, other nations are also battling this issue. In Turkey, researchers conducted a survey aimed at determining the eating patterns of Turkish youth. The results showed that just 15% of participants reported consuming the recommended daily amount of fruits and vegetables. Nearly one-third of participants said that they choose junk food or fast food as a daily snack, and the same number also reported having fast food once or more daily. Perhaps 85% of participants are not getting enough fruits and vegetables due to high consumption of junk or fast food. This supports the results of Davis and Carpenter's study, which showed that students with a high intake of fast food had a low intake of fruits and vegetables.

Researchers in Taiwan suggest that childhood consumption of fast food can have far-reaching effects that go beyond BMI rates. [They] conducted a nationwide survey to learn if fast food and soda consumption in children is associated with childhood obesity. Importantly, these researchers investigated whether fast food consumption impacts overall well being. They also wanted to know if fast food and soda consumption and the risk of being overweight have any relation to children's happiness. Consistent with other research, consumption of fast food and soda leads to children being overweight or obese; however, the study did not show any correlation to children's happiness.

Attacking the [obesity] epidemic from multiple angles will ensure the best chance of winning the battle of childhood obesity.

Action for the Future

Childhood obesity is a complicated issue, and its relationship to fast food is not simple. Many studies present clear results in showing that fast food consumption definitely has an influence on childhood obesity; other studies show that the issue is not so cut-and-dry. Regardless of the results of various studies, it seems clear that action needs to be taken in order to prevent this epidemic from continuing into future generations. Some researchers suggest that local policymakers need to become more involved in prohibiting new fast food restaurants from being built near schools or limiting the options available to children. Others suggest that education is paramount and needs to be given deep consideration. Still others emphasize that parents play a vital role in helping their children to develop healthy eating habits and food choices. These are all worthy suggestions, and just as childhood obesity results from a combination of factors, so shall the solution to this growing problem.

While various studies show that there are multiple angles to the issue of childhood obesity and its relationship to fast food, there are other areas that also need to be examined.

Many studies fail to explain the importance of exercise or mental stimulation. Other studies take away parental responsibility and instead place the blame on the clever marketing strategies of fast food restaurants. Researchers interested in childhood obesity give much attention to the nutritional aspect of the issue, but further research should explore and emphasize the roles of physical activity, mental stimulation, and parental influence. Attacking the epidemic from multiple angles will ensure the best chance of winning the battle of childhood obesity.

Fast Food Is Not a Major Cause of Childhood Obesity

Barry Popkin

Barry Popkin is a professor of nutrition at the University of North Carolina-Chapel Hill (UNC-CH), where he directs UNC-CH's Interdisciplinary Center for Obesity.

Fast food is often blamed for childhood obesity, but eating fast food is just a small part of poor eating habits that begin at home for many children and are reinforced at school with poor quality lunches. Fast food is just one element of an unhealthy diet that is high in sugar and processed foods and low in fruits, vegetables, and fresh foods. While reducing fast food consumption is desirable, children's day-to-day eating habits and their overall diets determine whether they will experience poor nutrition and obesity, not whether they eat fast food.

For several years, many have been quick to attribute rising fast-food consumption as the major factor causing rapid increases in childhood obesity. However a new study found that fast-food consumption is simply a byproduct of a much bigger problem: poor all-day-long dietary habits that originate in children's homes.

The study, titled "The association of fast food consumption with poor dietary outcomes and obesity among children: is it the fast food or the remainder of diet?," was produced by researchers at The University of North Carolina [UNC] at Chapel Hill's Gillings School of Global Public Health and published in the latest issue of *The American Journal of Clinical Nutrition.*

The study presented strong evidence that the children's diet beyond fast-food consumption is more strongly linked to poor nutrition and obesity.

The study's researchers found that children's consumption of fast food is only a small part of a much more pervasive dietary pattern that is fostered at an early age by children's parents and caregivers. The pattern includes few fruits and vegetables, relying instead on high amounts of processed food and sugar-sweetened beverages. These food choices also are reinforced in the meals students are offered at school.

Unfair Blame?

"This is really what is driving children's obesity," said Barry Popkin, PhD, W.R. Kenan Jr. Distinguished Professor of nutrition at UNC's Gillings School of Global Public Health, whose team led the study. "Eating fast foods is just one behavior that results from those bad habits. Just because children who eat more fast food are the most likely to become obese does not prove that calories from fast foods bear the brunt of the blame."

The study examined data acquired through the National Health and Nutrition Examination Survey (NHANES) between 2007 and 2010. Dietary intake, including whether foods and beverages were obtained in fast-food establishments or elsewhere, was evaluated in 4,466 children who were 2 years to 18 years of age. They were further categorized as being non-consumers of fast food (50 percent of the children), low consumers (less than or equal to 30 percent of calories from fast foods; 40 percent of the children), or high consumers (more than 30 percent of calories from fast foods; 10 percent of the children). The researchers then determined which factors were most related to dietary adequacy and risk for obesity.

What Else Are Kids Eating?

"The study presented strong evidence that the children's diet beyond fast-food consumption is more strongly linked to poor nutrition and obesity," said Jennifer Poti, doctoral candidate in UNC's Department of Nutrition and co-author of the study. "While reducing fast-food intake is important, the rest of a child's diet should not be overlooked."

Popkin said he is certainly no fan of fast-food consumption, but actually knowing where the problem originates is important if we are to invest in solutions that foster healthier habits, including reducing the consumption of sugary drinks and emphasizing more fresh vegetables and fruit.

"Children who rely on fast foods may tend to have parents who do not have the means, desire or time to purchase or prepare healthy foods at home," Popkin said. "This is really what is driving children's obesity and what needs to be addressed in any solution."

7

Parents Are Not to Blame for Their Children Being Obese

Abdul El-Sayed

Abdul El-Sayed is a social epidemiologist and physician in training. His research explores how social realities make people unhealthy. He is also a fellow at Dēmos, a nonpartisan public policy center in New York City.

Parents of obese children are often blamed for letting their kids become overweight. Critics say they should do more to control their children's diets and make them be more active. But it isn't that simple. The American food system subsidizes the commodity crops that are the main ingredients in the nation's high-calorie, high-sugar processed foods, allowing them to be sold far more cheaply than they otherwise would be. Individuals should not be blamed for obesity because it is a systemic problem that is heavily influenced by the politics of the food system; in effect, government agricultural policies subsidize obesity.

Recently, I wrote an open letter to [basketball player] LeBron James asking him to reconsider his endorsements with Coca-Cola and McDonald's and an article decrying [pop star] Beyoncé's recent $50 million contract with Pepsi. Reaction to the articles was mixed. Many supported them, recognizing the implicit influence that stars like LeBron and Beyoncé have on the consumption habits of impressionable children.

Abdul El-Sayed, "Are Parents Responsible for Childhood Obesity?," *The 2x2 Project*, Mailman School of Public Health, February 20, 2013. Copyright © 2013 Mailman School of Public Health. All rights reserved. Reproduced with permission.

Others were less supportive. They argued that rather than food companies and trend makers like LeBron and Beyoncé, children today are obese because their parents aren't doing a good job controlling their children's diets and coaching them to more active lifestyles.

But the numbers tell a different story.

Childhood obesity has tripled since 1980. Today, about 17 percent of American kids are obese and 25 percent are overweight. Such a drastic increase suggests that something has changed over the past 30 years. Getting to the bottom of what's causing the childhood obesity epidemic means figuring out what is changing.

And it's probably not parents.

American farm subsidies have largely underwritten the global food corporations that have come to be synonymous with obesity.

In fact, the numbers suggest that parents are more worried about obesity than ever before. A recent poll found that parents are increasingly worried about childhood obesity—it tied with illegal drug use as the most prominent concern among parents these days.

If parents haven't stopped caring about their kids' eating and exercise habits, what has changed?

Agricultural Subsidies Promote Obesity

In 1973, high commodity prices were devastating grain farmers throughout the central US. In response, the [Richard M.] Nixon administration initiated agricultural subsidies, artificially dropping the global price of corn and other grains. The reverberations of this move still echo throughout the food market—and have important implications for childhood obesity.

Subsidies keep the price of food, from beef to high-fructose corn syrup, artificially low. That, in turn, increases the number of people who eat foods containing these products both here in the US and abroad. American farm subsidies have largely underwritten the global food corporations that have come to be synonymous with obesity, like Coca-Cola, Pepsi, and McDonald's, by decreasing the cost of their starting materials and allowing them to sell their products at lower prices than the market would otherwise allow.

In that respect, what has changed is the environment within which parents are making decisions about food. Rather than being able to choose between several healthy, affordable options, today's post-subsidy world has rendered the most affordable options the least healthy, forcing parents' hands in favor of less nutritious diets for children, particularly in low-income settings.

The Broader Context

Blaming parents for childhood obesity is but one example in a larger narrative about how we falsely attribute the causes of obesity in our society. We blame individuals (or their guardians) for what seem to be simple personal choices to eat poorly and not exercise rather than thinking about the contextual incentives and disincentives they face that shape their behaviors.

More often than not, changing contexts are what change the behavior of large groups of people.

So where do LeBron and Beyoncé come in? Well, they didn't cause the obesity epidemic, either. But by underwriting corporations that are, they perpetuate the foodscape that has become so dangerous, accelerating the epidemic on the backs of impressionable children.

In the end, childhood obesity remains a concern for all of us (even Coca-Cola according to a recent ad they released). Rather than blame the obese (or their parents), it behooves us to think about how our environments may be shaping our decisions regarding diet and physical activity. And if the ultimate goal is [to] fix the problem, then we should look to its source: a food environment that is increasingly polluted with Coke and Big Macs that is limiting parents' food choices and fattening their children.

8

Unhealthy Food Should Not Be Marketed to Children

Prevention Institute

The Prevention Institute is a nonprofit that works to improve community health and well-being by focusing on effective prevention.

Marketing junk food to children is big business. The food and beverage industry spends about $2 billion a year targeting kids, often with ads for sugary drinks and junk food that are high in fat, sugar, and salt. Experts say it works: children who see food ads consume 45 percent more food than children who don't, and they eat fewer fruits, vegetables, and whole grains. Nearly 40 percent of children's diets are now made up of unhealthy fats and added sugars. Children should not be bombarded with ads for unhealthy foods that promote obesity and health problems like diabetes and high blood pressure. Congress should recommend that the food industry adopt guidelines for food marketing to children.

Experts agree that junk food is a huge contributor to skyrocketing rates of diabetes, high blood pressure, and even strokes. And food and beverage companies spend billions of dollars promoting unhealthy foods virtually everywhere kids go. The Interagency Working Group on Foods Marketed to Children (IWG) has proposed reasonable nutrition guidelines to help provide a model for companies that market to kids.

Unfortunately, the food industry and media companies are working to get Congress to stop the IWG from finalizing these sensible recommendations.

Read the facts below and watch "We're Not Buying It," a video that exposes deceptive marketing to children, debunks industry claims, and highlights the latest research. When we put children first, the plan of action is clear: companies should market the foods that keep kids healthy, not sugary cereals and other junk food. The IWG guidelines will help to do just that.

Facts About Children's Food Marketing

The food, beverage, and chain restaurant industry is targeting our children with intensive junk food marketing.

- The food and beverage industry spends approximately $2 billion per year marketing to children.

- The fast food industry spends more than $5 million every day marketing unhealthy foods to children.

- Kids watch an average of over ten food-related ads every day (nearly 4,000/year).

- Ad spending for interactive video games is projected to reach $1 billion by 2014, with six million 3–11 year olds visiting some form of virtual game online each month.

- Nearly all (98 percent) of food advertisements viewed by children are for products that are high in fat, sugar or sodium. Most (79 percent) are low in fiber.

If we continue on this path, the future health of our children is not so bright.

And it's working.. . .

- Nearly 40% of children's diets come from added sugars and unhealthy fats.

- Only 21% of youth age 6–19 eat the recommended five or more servings of fruits and vegetables each day.

- A mere 12% of grains consumed by children are whole.

- One study found that when children were exposed to television content with food advertising, they consumed 45 percent more food than children exposed to content with non-food adverting.

The food and beverage industry may say they're on the side of health, but their actions show otherwise.

- A 2011 review found that "company pledges to reduce food marketing of unhealthy products have failed to protect children <12 years for all types of marketing practices promoting such foods".

- Additionally, in 2010, an independent study documented that only 12 of 3039 children's meal combinations in fast food chain restaurants met established nutrition criteria for preschoolers; only 15 meals met nutrition criteria for older children.

- Each day, African-American children see twice as many calories advertised in fast-food commercials as White children.

- In 2010, the food and beverage industry spent over $40 billion lobbying Congress against several regulations including those that would decrease the marketing of unhealthy foods to kids, and potential soda taxes.

- A study conducted by Prevention Institute in 2007 found that over half of the most aggressively marketed children's foods advertising fruit on the packaging actually contain no fruit ingredients whatsoever.

- In 2011, a second study by researchers at Prevention Institute looked at packages with front of package labeling—symbols that identify healthier products—and found that 84% of products studied didn't meet basic nutritional standards.

If we continue on this path, the future health of our children is not so bright.

- Even five years after children have been exposed to promotions of unhealthy foods, researchers found that they purchased fewer fruits, vegetables and whole grains, but increased their consumption of fast foods, fried foods and sugar-sweetened beverages.

- According to the CDC [Centers for Disease Control and Prevention], if current trends continue, 1 of 3 U.S. adults will have diabetes by 2050.

- By 2030, healthcare costs attributable to poor diet and inactivity could range from $860 billion to $956 billion, which would account for 15.8 to 17.6 percent of total healthcare costs, or one in every six dollars spent on healthcare.

It's time to stand up to big food companies and protect the health of our kids. Ask President [Barack] Obama to insure that voluntary guidelines for food marketing to kids are put into place.

9

Food Marketing to Children Should Not Be Restricted

Ericka Andersen

Ericka Andersen is manager of digital media for The Heritage Foundation, a conservative think tank based in Washington, DC.

The so-called voluntary guidelines on children's food marketing proposed for the food and beverage industry are unreasonable and will penalize respectable companies simply because the government doesn't like what they are selling. Such a blatant censorship effort unfairly curtails the free speech rights of advertisers. The guidelines plan is not grounded in good science and it amounts to little more than creating a "government-regulated grocery list." There is no link between advertising and children's food choices, and the government should not try to regulate food marketing to children.

First Lady Michelle Obama's obsession with "childhood obesity" has bothered many since it began two years ago, especially those who think that White House nagging of parents should be reserved for more pressing issues. Now it is getting more serious, with food regulators starting to infringe on the free speech rights of advertisers.

In the latest upset, four federal agencies known as the Interagency Working Group (IWG) have delivered a plan to drastically censor food advertisers with products deemed to be "too high" in sodium, sugar, or fat that cater to any viewing audience between the ages of two and 11. These advertisers would lose key slots during some of America's most popular shows, like *American Idol, America's Got Talent,* and *Glee*—simply because the nanny state is "uncomfortable" with what they are selling.

The IWG, formed within the 2009 Omnibus Appropriations Act to study childhood obesity and offer possible solutions, has gone far beyond [its] descriptive reach. Now, perfectly reasonable companies may be penalized severely.

Voluntary in Name Only

The regulators plan to get away with this by disguising their rules as "voluntary guidelines." In reality, the guidelines are anything *but* optional, according to food manufacturers affected by them.

> *The free market and consumer choice is manipulated to fit a misplaced government agenda that doesn't solve the problem.*

As [The Heritage Foundation's] Diane Katz explains:

> The restrictions are voluntary in name only. Food manufacturers can hardly ignore "recommendations" from the very federal agencies that exercise regulatory authority over their every move. It is akin to a cop asking for ID or to search one's vehicle: While the law treats such citizen cooperation as voluntary, most individuals would not view it as such, nor would the police look kindly on anyone who denies their requests.

It's not just Twinkies and cookies that will be affected, either. Anything deemed to have a little too much sodium or fat will be tested under the new rules, including foods whose very production requires a high sodium content (like pickles) and those that are naturally high fat (like peanuts).

As Katz wrote, "Nutritional staples such as Cheerios, peanut butter, and yogurt are verboten under the proposed standards, which effectively constitute a government-regulated grocery list."

The regulations hit traditional favorites where it hurts. In turn, the free market and consumer choice is manipulated to fit a misplaced government agenda that doesn't solve the problem.

Even if the feds are well-intentioned, their action plan isn't grounded in reliable research. The whole point of the regulations is to curb the growing epidemic of childhood obesity—but the Institute of Medicine found no link between advertisements and children's food choices.

Less Advertising but More Obesity

According to Katz, children have seen about 50 percent less food advertising in the last six years than before that time—yet obesity rates continue to climb. Former FDA [Food and Drug Administration] Commissioner Dr. Mark McClellan attributes the obesity problem to "physical inactivity"—not caloric intake. In fact, McClellan noted that children's calorie intake has remained about the same for the last 20 years.

Not only do regulations hinder the market and censor speech; they hurt the businesses behind the labels. Sara Lee CEO [chief executive officer] Christopher J. Fraleigh recently spoke on the overextended regulations, which will hurt his business in particular:

> A turkey sandwich made with Sara Lee fat-free lean turkey meat, we would not be able to advertise that on venues, be it the Superbowl or anything that would have a significant child audience, because the product is a little bit too high in sodium. . . . Current regulation of advertising toward children is a perfect example of regulation that just goes way too far.

The [President Barack] Obama Administration's food regulators think that if you give them an inch, they can take a mile. But when free speech is on the cutting board, they will certainly hear from the people, and the people will not stand for it.

10

Early Intervention Works to Combat Childhood Obesity

Taryn Morrissey et al.

Along with Taryn Morrissey, four other authors from the Office of the Assistant Secretary for Planning and Education, US Department of Health and Human Services, contributed to this viewpoint. Morrissey is an assistant professor of public administration and policy at the School of Public Affairs at American University in Washington, DC. Her work focuses on examining and improving public policies for vulnerable children.

Early care and education programs promote a wide variety of positive outcomes for children, including lower rates of obesity. The Head Start program, for example, has been shown to decrease the body mass index (BMI) of children over the course of a year's participation. The Head Start program also demonstrates long-term impacts on obesity, showing "large reductions" over time. Experts agree that preschool intervention brings the best long-term results for reducing obesity and promoting other positive outcomes, such as language skills and school readiness.

Research consistently finds that high-quality early care and education (ECE) programs promote children's school readiness and other positive outcomes. This brief describes what's known about the short- and long-term impacts of large public (i.e., at-scale) ECE programs in the United States for children prior to kindergarten entry—including what key features of programs lead to the best outcomes, and how to sustain program benefits as children grow older. This brief does not include the many smaller ECE programs, including model or demonstration programs in the U.S. and abroad, that have also been evaluated; please see other reports for information on the short- and long-term impacts of these programs.

What Are the Short-Term Impacts?

Research indicates that one or more years of high-quality, developmentally appropriate early care and education (ECE) improves a range of children's outcomes, including language, literacy, and numeracy skills, when measured at the end of the program or soon after. These findings are consistent across small demonstration programs, such as the well-known Perry Preschool and Abecedarian programs, which have shown very large effects, as well as among large-scale public programs such as public pre-K and Head Start programs. The large-scale public programs have shown positive but more modest short-term effects, but they were also, in general, less costly or intensive, and served a broader range of children.

> *Head Start may also show long-term impacts on health outcomes, particularly large reductions in obesity and on the likelihood of smoking.*

Relatively recent research on the impact of high-quality prekindergarten programs on children's outcomes is quite strong, providing evidence for both short- and long-term impacts of meaningful magnitude. Pre-K yields large short-term effects on academic measures of school readiness (e.g., cognition, language), and some studies show that pre-K programs improve social-emotional development. For example, research on Oklahoma's universal prekindergarten program in Tulsa indicates that children who attended pre-K were advanced on pre-reading skills by 9 months, pre-writing skills by 7 months, and pre-math skills by 5 months, compared to similar children who did not participate. The Tulsa study also found more modest gains in social-emotional development, including higher attentiveness and lower timidity (but not differences in other aspects of problem behavior). Likewise, a recent study of Boston's city-wide prekindergarten program found moderate to large effects on children's language, literacy, numeracy, and math skills, and smaller impacts on children's executive functioning and emotion recognition. In Tennessee's pre-K program, participating children scored about one-third of a standard deviation higher on cognitive tests than nonparticipants at the end of the pre-K year. Further, research indicates that Head Start participation is associated with increased receipt of health screenings, immunizations, and dental exams, and a small decrease in body mass index (BMI) over the course of the academic year (full-day programs were found to contribute to larger reductions in obesity than half-day programs, by about 4 percentage points). The recent Head Start Impact Study (HSIS) found small to modest benefits for school readiness skills (e.g., language, cognition) and social-emotional skills (e.g., hyperactive and withdrawn behaviors for the 3-year-old cohort only) at the end of the Head Start year, although by 1st and 3rd grade, these impacts were mixed or mostly diminished.

What Are the Long-Term Impacts?

While studies consistently find that ECE participation has positive impacts on children's outcomes at program's end, only a few have longitudinal data available to assess long-term outcomes.

In general, differences attributable to program participation on measures of achievement diminish or disappear during elementary and secondary schooling. However, despite the convergence of scores on measures of academic achievement, multiple studies show long-term effects on important life outcomes in late adolescence or early adulthood. For example, children who attend Head Start have higher rates of high school completion, college attendance, and employment, as well as decreases in behavior problems, grade retention, and criminal activity, when compared to similar children who did not attend Head Start. Overall, Head Start attendance results in an increase of nearly one-quarter of a standard deviation (.23 SD) across an index of outcomes, equivalent to about one-third of the gap between Head Start participants and other children that existed prior to participation. The projected gains in earnings associated with program attendance more than offset the costs of the program, resulting in a positive benefit/cost ratio for Head Start. Head Start may also show long-term impacts on health outcomes, particularly large reductions in obesity and on the likelihood of smoking.

While this study found no difference in test scores during middle childhood, Head Start participants were much less likely to repeat a grade or be diagnosed with a learning disability.

Documentation Is Lacking

Because documenting long-term impacts require longitudinal studies and measures taken decades after participation, to date, we lack information on the long-term impacts of public pre-K programs. A small number of model, intensive ECE programs with available longitudinal data demonstrate large long-term impacts. For example, evaluations of two well-known ECE programs, the Perry Preschool and the Carolina Abecedarian projects, show very large initial impacts on educational achievement, and very large effects on schooling and earnings during adulthood. Likewise, the Chicago Child-Parent Centers study also shows substantial short-term effects on educational achievement, plus long-term reductions in crime and substance abuse and long-term improvements in high school graduation rates and adult earnings.

What Is the "Fadeout" or "Catch-up" Phenomena?

"Fadeout" of ECE impacts refers to the diminishing effect sizes of ECE attendance on children's test scores over time, as children age. One possible explanation for fadeout may be that non-participating children actually "catch up" over time, suggesting that the term "convergence" may be more appropriate. Some research suggests that fadeout may occur at a faster rate among children who go on to attend lower-quality schools although other recent research suggests fadeout occurs at a slower rate in low-achieving schools. The initial achievement gains from Head Start also fadeout at a faster rate for African-American children, who (on average) attend lower-quality schools.

The pattern of (1) initial impacts on test scores, (2) convergence or "fadeout" over time, and (3) significant long-term gains on important adult outcomes was found in evaluations of Perry Preschool, Carolina Abecedarian, Head Start, and even the Tennessee STAR kindergarten class size reduction experiment, indicating that the convergence of test scores and yet long-term gains in adult outcomes is a robust pattern in ECE interventions. In the case of Head Start, children who exhibited the greatest fadeout of ECE impacts actually experienced the largest impacts as adults. Specifically, the children who showed large initial test score gains at ages five and six and diminished impacts at ages 11 and 14 exhibited larger outcomes in adulthood, relative to other Head Start participants, suggesting that initial test score gains may be a better predictor of long-term outcomes than interim test scores. Further, while this study found no difference in test scores during middle childhood, Head Start participants were much less likely to repeat a grade or be diagnosed with a learning disability. This suggests other indicators may be more useful than interim test scores as predictors of long-run impacts. Moreover, these indicators, such as grade retention, often have cost implications themselves.

Stimulating, supportive teacher-child interactions constitute the most important aspect of a high-quality ECE program.

How Does Early Childhood Participation Help?

Much remains unknown about the mechanisms underlying this pattern of convergence, as it is possible that there are different causal pathways for the short- and long-term effects. One possible pathway through which ECE programs may have long-term impacts is through changes in children's behavior, particularly in their approaches to learning such as increased self-regulation and attention skills, that they carry through life. Another potential mechanism through which ECE programs may have long-term impacts is through changes in parenting quality or practices. For example, secondary analysis of data from the HSIS revealed persistent impacts on parents' involvement with children's schooling several years later. Additionally, Head Start, as well as the small model ECE programs, place programmatic emphasis on increased parental education and involvement. Because socioeconomic differences in the home environment, parenting, and parents' involvement in education account for a substantial portion of the income achievement gap, changes in parenting could help narrow this gap. Moreover, evidence suggests that there may be beneficial spillover effects of Head Start participation on young siblings, which may be the result of changes in parenting. Finally, as mentioned above, the quality of the K-12 schools that ECE participants attend may help sustain earlier gains, although the research on this is mixed.

Do All Children Benefit from Early Intervention?

Research on universal ECE programs in Tulsa, Boston, and Tennessee suggests that attending high-quality ECE benefits all children, including children of all racial, ethnic, and income groups. However, pre-K attendance is especially beneficial to the most disadvantaged children and children from certain ethnic-minority groups. For example, in Tulsa, compared to their control group peers, children from poor families were 11 months ahead, children from near-poor families were 10 months ahead, and children from middle-class families were 7 months ahead upon entering kindergarten after attending pre-K. Likewise, in Boston, both children from low-income (defined as eligible for free- or reduced-price lunch) and middle-class families experienced gains in language, literacy, and mathematics outcomes, but low-income children exhibited greater gains. Further, gains in inhibitory control and attention shifting were accrued almost entirely by low-income children. In both Boston and Oklahoma, Latino/Hispanic children exhibited larger gains in letter-word identification from pre-K attendance than their Asian, Black, or White peers. Similarly, in Tennessee, English Language Learners (most of whom were Hispanic) exhibited larger cognitive gains than their native English-speaking peers.

What Makes a Good Program?

ECE programs are often "packages" of services in that they are multi-faceted, and serve children and families in a variety of different ways, making it difficult to determine exactly which components are important to outcomes (e.g., full- or part-day programming for children, specific classroom or teacher preparation activities, parent education or involvement components). However, we know that stimulating, supportive teacher-child interactions constitute the most important aspect of a high-quality ECE program. Structural features of the environment, or features that can be directly regulated by program requirements or standards, such as group size, teacher-child ratio, and teacher education and professional development, can facilitate—but do not assure—that such positive teacher-child interactions will occur. The use of an evidence-based, developmentally-focused and intensive curriculum, the inclusion of strong instructional support or professional development (e.g., in-class coaching or mentoring), and more classroom time spent on task are also common features of effective programs.

11

Physical Activity Plays a Key Role in Reducing Childhood Obesity

Leann L. Birch, Lynn Parker, and Annina Burns

Leann L. Birch is a professor and director of the Center for Childhood Obesity Research at Pennsylvania State University. She was chair of the study from which this viewpoint is taken. Annina Burns directed the study until February 2011, and Lynn Parker served as study director from March 2011 forward.

Increasing physical activity and reducing sedentary behavior are important for preventing weight gain, and they are key strategies in the effort to reduce childhood obesity. Infants, toddlers, and preschool-age children should have the opportunity to be physically active throughout the day. Childcare facilities should be required to ensure that is the case and should limit the use of equipment, such as strollers or high chairs, that restrict the mobility of children. Health and education professionals who work with children should be trained in ways to reduce sedentary behavior and increase physical activity. Adults control how young children spend their time and are responsible for making healthy decisions on their behalf.

Over the past 20 years, society has changed in multiple ways that have reduced the demand for physical activity and increased the time spent in sedentary pursuits. These trends have been evident even in the youngest children. It is well documented that many children under age 5 fail to meet physical activity guidelines established by expert panels. The relationships among weight status, physical activity, and sedentary behavior are not yet fully understood in young children, but the limited research on this issue is growing. Some evidence suggests that higher levels of physical activity are associated with a reduced risk of excessive weight gain over time in young children, and similar evidence is more extensive in older children and adults. Additional prevention-oriented research to study the relationship between physical activity and risk of excessive weight over time in children is important.

Child care providers and early childhood educators [should] provide infants, toddlers, and preschool children with opportunities to be physically active throughout the day.

Increasing physical activity and reducing sedentary behavior are logical and accepted strategies for maintaining energy balance and preventing excessive weight gain. Recent evidence-based publications from government agencies, often developed using recommendations from scientific panels, affirm the importance of physical activity in reducing the risk of excessive weight gain. For example, the *Dietary Guidelines for Americans 2010* counsels Americans two years of age and older that "Strong evidence supports that regular participation in physical activity also helps people maintain a healthy weight and prevent excess weight gain." *The Surgeon General's Vision for a Healthy and Fit Nation* argues that "Physical activity can help control weight, reduce risk for many diseases (heart disease and some cancers), strengthen your bones and muscles, improve your mental health, and increase your chances of living longer." The 2008 *Physical Activity Guidelines for Americans*, targeted to children over six years of age and adults, states,

"Regular physical activity in children and adolescents promotes a healthy body weight and body composition."

Policy and Practice Recomendations

This chapter thus presents policy and practice recommendations aimed at increasing physical activity and decreasing sedentary behaviors in young children. Specifically, the recommendations in this chapter are intended to (1) increase young children's physical activity in child care and other settings, (2) decrease young children's sedentary behaviors in child care and other settings, and (3) help adults adopt policies and practices that will increase physical activity and decrease sedentary behavior in young children. Each of these recommendations includes specific action steps for its implementation. Recommendations for infants are included in an effort to highlight the need to begin obesity prevention practices in early life. The recommendations in this chapter target child care regulatory agencies, child care providers, early childhood educators, communities, colleges and universities, and national organizations for health and education professionals, urging them to collectively adopt policies and practices that will promote physical activity and limit sedentary behavior in young children.

Goal: Increase Physical Activity in Young Children

Recommendation 3-1: Child care regulatory agencies should require child care providers and early childhood educators to provide infants, toddlers, and preschool children with opportunities to be physically active throughout the day.

For infants, potential actions include:

- providing daily opportunities for infants to move freely under adult supervision to explore their indoor and outdoor environments;

- engaging with infants on the ground each day to optimize adult-infant interactions; and

- providing daily "tummy time" (time in the prone position) for infants less than 6 months of age.

Child care providers and early childhood educators [should] allow infants, toddlers, and preschoolers to move freely by limiting the use of equipment that restricts infants' movement.

For toddlers and preschool children potential actions include:

- providing opportunities for light, moderate, and vigorous physical activity for at least 15 minutes per hour while children are in care;

- providing daily outdoor time for physical activity when possible;

- providing a combination of developmentally appropriate structured and unstructured physical activity experiences;

- joining children in physical activity;

- integrating physical activity into activities designed to promote children's cognitive and social development;

- providing an outdoor environment with a variety of portable play equipment, a secure perimeter, some shade, natural elements, an open grassy area, varying surfaces and terrain, and adequate space per child;

- providing an indoor environment with a variety of portable play equipment and adequate space per child;

- providing opportunities for children with disabilities to be physically active, including equipment that meets the current standards for accessible design under the Americans with Disabilities Act;

- avoiding punishing children for being physically active; and

- avoiding withholding physical activity as punishment. . . .

Recommendation 3-2: The community and its built environment should promote physical activity for children from birth to age 5.
Potential actions include:

- ensuring that indoor and outdoor recreation areas encourage all children, including infants, to be physically active;

- allowing public access to indoor and outdoor recreation areas located in public education facilities; and

- ensuring that indoor and outdoor recreation areas provide opportunities for physical activity that meet current standards for accessible design under the Americans with Disabilities Act (ADA). . . .

Goal: Decrease Sedentary Behavior in Young Children

Recommendation 3-3: Child care regulatory agencies should require child care providers and early childhood educators to allow infants, toddlers, and preschoolers to move freely by limiting the use of equipment that restricts infants' movement and by implementing appropriate strategies to ensure that the amount of time toddlers and preschoolers spend sitting or standing still is limited.
Potential actions include:

- using cribs, car seats, and high chairs for their primary purpose only—cribs for sleeping, car seats for vehicle travel, and high chairs for eating;

- limiting the use of equipment such as strollers, swings, and bouncer seats/chairs for holding infants while they are awake;

- implementing activities for toddlers and preschoolers that limit sitting or standing to no more than 30 minutes at a time; and

- using strollers for toddlers and preschoolers only when necessary. . . .

It is the cumulative impact of decisions made by adults that shapes the development of the bodies and minds of young children.

Goal: Help Adults Increase Children's Physical Activity and Decrease Sedentary Behavior in Young Children

Recommendation 3-4: Health and education professionals providing guidance to parents of young children and those working with young children should be trained in ways to increase children's physical activity and decrease their sedentary behavior, and in how to counsel parents about their children's physical activity.

Potential actions include:

- Colleges and universities that offer degree programs in child development, early childhood education nutrition, nursing, physical education, public health, and medicine requiring content within coursework on how to increase physical activity and decrease sedentary behavior in young children.

- Child care regulatory agencies encouraging child care and early childhood education programs to seek consultation yearly from an expert in early childhood physical activity.

- Child care regulatory agencies requiring child care providers and early childhood educators to be trained in ways to encourage physical activity and decrease sedentary behavior in young children through certification and continuing education.

- National organizations that provide certification and continuing education for dietitians, physicians, nurses, and other health professionals (including the American Dietetic Association and the American Academy of Pediatrics) including content on how to counsel parents about children's physical activity and sedentary behaviors.

Messages about physical activity and sedentary behavior ... must be consistent across settings—from the pediatrician's office, to the WIC clinic, to the child care center.

Adults Are the Key to Change

Adults control where and how children under age 5 spend their time. These decisions influence the variety, frequency, and intensity of children's movement experiences and thus their motor development, energy expenditure, and body weight. For example, whether an awake infant in the home is spending time constrained in a car seat or prone and moving freely on the floor may have implications for that infant's gross motor development, movement, and energy expenditure. Whether a toddler or preschooler at home spends time watching television or playing outdoors may have similar implications. These decisions about allocation of time across activities also affect children's cognitive, social, and emotional development. Thus it is the cumulative impact of decisions made by adults that shapes the development of the bodies and minds of young children.

Of all the adults who make decisions about activities for infants, toddlers, and preschoolers, it is parents (or guardians) who have the greatest influence because children at this age still spend the majority of their time in their parents' care. This is true even for children in full-day child care or preschool. Therefore, how children spend the time they are with their parents and the nature of the physical environment in the home are two key leverage points for preventing obesity from birth to age 5. Parents establish the household policies and practices in these two areas. Therefore, for public policy to affect these areas, it must reach parents.

Parents seek advice in raising their children from those they trust. Outside of friends and family, the professionals they often trust include the following: health care providers; child care providers; early childhood educators; and those working in home visiting programs, the Special Supplemental Nutrition Program for Women, Infants, and Children (WIC), and U.S. Department of Agriculture (USDA) Cooperative Extension programs. These professionals function within institutions, programs, and professional organizations that can develop policies and practices that influence the content and frequency of professionals' communication with parents on a number of issues affecting children's physical activity.

The Role of Professionals

The first two goals of this chapter involve recommendations designed to alter settings outside the home by changing physical environments and the ways adults in those settings interact with children and allocate children's time across activities. It would be ideal for parents to implement many of these same recommendations at home. Parents can be aided in this effort by the professionals from whom they already seek advice about parenting. For parents to be receptive to this advice, they must feel encouraged by these professionals rather than blamed, and the advice must be practical and compatible with the parents' values. Messages about physical activity and sedentary behavior also must be consistent across settings—from the pediatrician's office, to the WIC clinic, to the child care center.

Finally, professionals can empower parents to change children's environments and activities outside the home to encourage physical activity and decrease sedentary behavior. Parents need the support of professionals to advocate for these changes in their communities, especially in settings where their children receive child care and early childhood education. Parents' expression of their opinions can change the indoor and outdoor environments in all these settings, the ways in which nonparental adults interact with their children, and the kinds of activities their children engage in while away from home.

12

Declines in Childhood Obesity Are Greatly Exaggerated

Bryn Martyna

Bryn Martyna is a former Skadden Fellow and staff attorney at the National Center for Youth Law, a California-based nonprofit that uses the law to improve the lives of poor children. She now works for the Wisconsin Supreme Court.

Although media outlets widely cited a relatively high percentage (43 percent) when they reported that the obesity rate for children aged two to five dropped dramatically, the change has actually only been 5.5 percentage points. Additionally, children two to five years old made up a very small portion of the study in question, so it is likely that the decline is even smaller than that. The study did include some encouraging findings about childhood obesity, but when the significance of data is exaggerated in the media it affects the public's perception of an issue and can even provide false direction for public health officials and professionals.

A recent *New York Times* front-page article touted a dramatic 43-percent drop in obesity rates for children ages two to five from 2003–04 to 2011–12. This article, along with others in many other major news outlets, was accompanied by much celebration and speculation about the possible cause of this apparently significant decline.

However, a closer look at the study, appearing in the *Journal of the American Medical Association* (*JAMA*) on February 26 [2014], reveals a more complicated story. Even after a closer look, it does appear likely that the rate is decreasing for two to five year olds, it is not as straightforward or compelling a story as the headlines would lead you to believe.

The actual decrease was from 13.9 percent to 8.4 percent over the eight-year period, but most major news outlets emphasized the relative percentage (43 percent) instead of the absolute decrease of 5.5 percentage points. However, there are a few reasons to treat even the absolute decrease with caution.

It is likely there has been some decline [in childhood obesity], but the significance and size of the decline is less certain.

First, as the authors of the *JAMA* study noted somewhat obtusely in the report, when looking at a small subgroup of a large data set, relatively large percentage variations over time are more likely to appear. Simply put, when there are fewer numbers, there is more likely to be some statistical "noise"— differences that look significant but do not reach a level of statistical significance. Here, two to five year olds were less than ten percent of the data set analyzed, which looked at only 9,120 people total. This is why a higher standard for statistical significance is often used, although the authors note that they did not use this higher standard.

No Clear Trend in the Data

Second, there is not a clear trend from year to year when looking at more data points over the eight-year period. According to the same data source used for the report, the obesity rate for two to five year olds declined by 23 percent between 2003–04 and 2005–06, and then rose by 19.8 percent between 2007–08 and 2009–10. Thus, while the 43 percent decline is technically there, when considered in context, it is not as clearly evidence of a steady trend of decline.

This is not to say that the information in the report does not offer any indication that the obesity rate is declining for two to five year olds. Using confidence intervals at each end— the range of statistical possibilities rather than the most likely point near the middle—the eight-year change comes out somewhere between a 7 percent increase and a 66 percent decrease. In essence, this means it is likely there has been some decline, but the significance and size of the decline is less certain.

Finally, the numbers should be considered in the context of the entire report. The report clearly stated that overall, the obesity rates for adults and children in the United States are statistically unchanged between 2003–04 and 2011–12.

Media Coverage Is Skewed

After the initial excitement, some news outlets became critical of the focus on the 43 percent drop. On February 28, *Slate* put it bluntly: "The obesity rate for children has not plummeted, despite what the *New York Times* tells you." They highlighted the various concerns with the data, drawing a wide range of conclusions based on those criticisms.

The *New York Times*, among others, speculated about the possible causes of the decline, citing a decrease in children's consumption of calories through sugary beverages, increased breast feeding, and a combination of local, state, and federal policies focused on decreasing childhood obesity, among other factors.

The conservative news outlet, *The New Republic*, criticized the results, arguing that there is no obesity epidemic, so "stop applauding Michelle Obama for reducing it." The article acknowledges that no one has any idea why obesity rates have

stopped increasing, but also claims that public health interventions have uniformly failed, citing another *JAMA* study
from 1996.

---

*The findings in this case appear to have been blown out
of proportion in the initial reporting, and then again by
commentators using them to make a point.*

Whether these types of exaggerated findings are used to
support government efforts to reduce obesity or defeat them,
Slate adeptly highlighted the larger ramifications of allowing
these types of headlines to drive policy:

A far bigger issue is that studies like these, and the headlines that result, drive the discussion about public health and
policy in this country. The media seizes on sexy results, ampli-
fies them without due skepticism, and the public is misled.
This can impact billions of dollars allocated to campaigns
meant to capitalize on the supposed implications of scientific
studies. It's hardly an academic footnote in this case. Commentators are already attempting to adduce the reasons for
the decline in obesity in this age, pointing to the dietary
changes in preschool menus, awareness campaigns, and exercise programs that specifically target tots.

The findings in this case appear to have been blown out of
proportion in the initial reporting, and then again by commentators using them to make a point. While there may be
some reason to be cautiously optimistic that dietary changes,
awareness campaigns, and exercise programs are having some
positive impact, this should not be treated as anywhere near
the final word on the matter. It provides somewhat tangential
support for the idea that they are helping, and no reason to
conclude they are not. Efforts to tease out the impacts of various efforts to reduce childhood obesity should continue, as
should the efforts to reduce obesity themselves.

Children in Poverty Were Overlooked

The recent *JAMA* study did not separate out analysis for children in poverty. However, other studies have offered greater insight, drawing from a much larger data sample, as to whether obesity rates are declining for children in poverty. The recent *JAMA* report analyzed data for only 9,120 participants total. In 2012, *JAMA* published a report analyzing data from the Pediatric Nutrition Surveillance System (PedNSS), which includes almost 50 percent of children eligible for federally funded maternal and child health and nutrition programs. The analysis included 26.7 million children ages 2 through 4 years from 30 states and the District of Columbia.

That study found a slight decline in obesity among preschool-aged children living in low-income families in the United States. They observed a decrease in the prevalence of obesity from 15.21 percent in 2003 to 14.94 percent in 2010, and a decrease in the prevalence of extreme obesity from 2.22 percent in 2003 to 2.07 percent in 2010.

The authors took a much more measured approach in reporting their findings:

"To our knowledge, this is the first national study to show that the prevalence of obesity and extreme obesity among young U.S. children may have begun to decline," the authors write. "The results of this study indicate modest recent progress of obesity prevention among young children."

The Bigger Picture

The recent data, even if they give some reason to be encouraged that obesity rates have stopped increasing, or are even on the decline for some sub-groups, must be considered in context. There is a still a considerable obesity problem in this country, by any measure. The percentage of children aged 6–11 years in the United States who were obese increased from 7% in 1980 to nearly 18% in 2012. As the report itself concluded: "Obesity prevalence remains high and thus it is important to continue surveillance."

We gain little from exaggerating the significance of data. If overstated results lead to complacency, premature abandonment of efforts to reduce childhood obesity, or failure to consider the many complex factors contributing to an important health issue, that would truly be a shame.

13

Children Whose Parents Divorce Are More Likely to Be Obese

Steven Reinberg

Steven Reinberg is a senior staff reporter for HealthDay, a syndicated news service specializing in health topics.

Researchers in Norway have discovered that children—especially boys—whose parents divorce are more likely to become obese, although they cannot show that divorce is the cause. The study found that children overall were 54 percent more likely to be obese and 89 percent more likely to carry their weight in their bellies than children whose parents were not divorced; for boys, the percentages were even higher—63 percent and 104 percent, respectively. Researchers speculate that contributing factors could include emotional eating, single parents being too busy to cook nutritious meals, reduced hours of parental supervision, and disruption of healthy eating and sleeping routines.

Kids face many challenges when their parents divorce, and their struggles often include excessive weight gain, new research suggests.

Boys are especially prone to excess weight in the wake of divorce, according to the study of 3,000 third-graders in Norway.

These boys were 63 percent more likely to be overweight or obese than boys whose parents stayed married, the researchers found. They were also 104 percent more likely to be abdominally obese.

"Knowing which factors are associated with childhood overweight and obesity is crucial, and is the first step toward being able to prevent it," said lead researcher Anna Biehl, of the Norwegian Institute of Public Health in Oslo.

From less supervision at home to family stress, experts say there are many possible reasons why kids in divorced families may pack on weight.

The researchers cautioned that they found an association between divorce and weight gain, but can't say divorce is the cause. They also didn't account for how long parents had been divorced or lifestyle factors such as diet and exercise.

Divorce and childhood obesity are increasingly common in developed nations. In the United States, obesity has more than doubled in children and quadrupled in teenagers in the past 30 years, according to the U.S. Centers for Disease Control and Prevention. Children who are obese are at higher risk for serious health problems such as diabetes and heart disease as they grow older.

Many Possible Reasons for Obesity-Divorce Link

From less supervision at home to family stress, experts say there are many possible reasons why kids in divorced families may pack on weight.

"Divorced families sometimes turn to maladaptive behaviors for coping and some of that is emotional eating or decreased activity," said Sara Rivero-Conil, a child psychologist at Miami Children's Hospital, who wasn't involved in the study.

Single parents might feel too pressed for time to cook nutritious meals. "Some may resort to unhealthy foods because they are quicker [to prepare]," she said. "Or a parent who has the kids on a weekend may want to indulge them."

Boys could be under extra stress as they try to take on the role of the "man in the house," she added. "We see that when mom has full or shared custody," Rivero-Conil said.

It helps to keep to a normal routine during and after a divorce and to maintain a healthy environment, including diet and exercise, Rivero-Conil said.

Also, if you eat together, your kids are less likely to be obese, she said. "Take that 30 minutes to have breakfast or dinner with your children to show them what healthy eating is like," she added.

Dr. David Katz, director of the Yale University Prevention Research Center in New Haven, Conn., thinks the risk of weight gain after divorce is one more piece of the obesity epidemic.

"For the majority of people living in the modern world—adults and children alike—getting fat is easy, and remaining lean is hard," Katz said.

Boys Seem Especially Vulnerable

Divorce may make gaining weight even easier, especially for boys, he said.

"Divorce might reduce the hours of parental supervision," said Katz. "It might introduce severe stress. It might result in financial hardship. It might shift attention away from health and food choice. It might invite more emotional eating by affected adults as well as children. These are just a few likely mechanisms."

Divorce likely compounds increasingly widespread vulnerabilities to obesity, he said.

"Perhaps specific attention to the mechanisms of weight gain after divorce may be warranted, so that those affected are empowered to resist," Katz said.

"But probably more important is the work required to turn the tide of pandemic obesity overall, by empowering families to eat well and be active as a matter of routine," he added.

For the study, published online June 4 [2014] in *BMJ Open*, Biehl's team collected data on boys and girls in 127 schools across Norway. These 8- and 9-year-old children were part of the 2010 Norwegian Child Growth Study.

The researchers found that 19 percent of the children were overweight or obese and nearly 9 percent were abdominally obese.

Overall, children of divorced parents were 54 percent more likely to be overweight or obese, and 89 percent more likely to have abdominal obesity compared to children whose parents stayed married, the study found.

The difference was especially apparent for boys. A similar weight pattern was seen for daughters of divorce, but the researchers said it was not statistically significant.

Organizations to Contact

The editors have compiled the following list of organizations concerned with the issues debated in this book. The descriptions are derived from materials provided by the organizations. All have publications or information available for interested readers. The list was compiled on the date of publication of the present volume; the information provided here may change. Be aware that many organizations take several weeks or longer to respond to inquiries, so allow as much time as possible.

Academy of Nutrition and Dietetics (AND)
120 S Riverside Plaza, Suite 2000, Chicago, IL   60606
(800) 877-1600
e-mail: media@eatright.org
website: www.eatright.org

The Academy of Nutrition and Dietetics (AND) is the world's largest organization of food and nutrition professionals. The organization is committed to improving the nation's health and advancing the profession of dietetics through research, education, and advocacy. AND provides reliable and evidence-based nutrition information for the public, acts as the accrediting agency for graduate and undergraduate nutrition education curricula, credentials dietetics professionals, and advocates for public policy issues that affect consumers and the practice of dietetics. The *Journal of the Academy of Nutrition and Dietetics* is the group's official research publication, and *Food and Nutrition* is its magazine for members and professionals.

American Academy of Pediatrics (AAP)
141 Northwest Point Blvd., Elk Grove Village, IL   60007-1098
(847) 434-4000 • fax: (847) 434-8000
website: www.aap.org

The American Academy of Pediatrics (AAP) is an organization of pediatricians committed to the optimal physical, mental, and social health and well-being for all infants, children, adolescents, and young adults. AAP offers continuing medical education programs for pediatricians and its website features policy statements, clinical reports, clinical practice guidelines, and technical reports. *AAP News* is the official newsmagazine of the AAP, while *Pediatrics* is the official journal.

Association for Size Diversity and Health (ASDAH)

PO Box 3093, Redwood City, CA 94064

(877) 576-1102

website: www.sizediversityandhealth.org

The Association for Size Diversity and Health (ASDAH) is an international professional organization comprised of individuals who are committed to the Health At Every Size principles. ASDAH's mission is to promote education, research, and services that enhance health and well-being and are free from weight-based assumptions and weight discrimination. The group's website features information about the Health At Every Size approach as well as a blog, research papers, and other relevant publications and resources.

Center for Science in the Public Interest (CSPI)

1220 L St. NW, Suite 300, Washington, DC 20005

(202) 332-9110 • fax: (202) 265-4954

e-mail: cspi@cspinet.org

website: http://cspinet.org

The mission of the Center for Science in the Public Interest (CSPI) is to educate the public and advocate for government policies that are consistent with scientific evidence on nutrition, food safety, health, environmental protection, and other issues. The CSPI's goals include eliminating junk food in schools, eliminating partially hydrogenated oil in the American diet, improving food safety laws, and advocating for more healthy, plant-based, environmentally friendly diets, among other issues. The CSPI publishes a monthly newsletter, *Nutrition Action Healthletter*.

Centers for Disease Control and Prevention, Division of Nutrition, Physical Activity, and Obesity (DNPAO)

1600 Clifton Rd., Atlanta, GA 30333
(800) 232-4636
e-mail: cdcinfo@cdc.gov
website: www.cdc.gov/nccdphp/dnpao/index.html

The Division of Nutrition, Physical Activity, and Obesity (DNPAO) is part of the Centers for Disease Control and Prevention (CDC), an agency of the US Department of Health and Human Services. The DNPAO works to prevent and control obesity, chronic disease, and other health conditions through advocating regular physical activity and good nutrition. The division supports state health departments, provides funding to reduce obesity and obesity-related diseases, and supports research to enhance the effectiveness of physical activity and nutrition programs. The DNPAO website offers myriad publications on obesity, as well as such useful data as state obesity rates and physical activity rates.

Eunice Kennedy Shriver National Institute of Child Health and Human Development (NICHD)

31 Center Dr., Bldg. 31, Room 2A32
Bethesda, MD 20892-2425
(800) 370-2943 • fax: (866) 760-5947
e-mail: NICHDInformationResourceCenter@mail.nih.gov
website: www.nichd.nih.gov

The National Institute of Child Health and Human Development (NICHD), part of the National Institutes of Health, conducts and supports research on topics related to the health and development of children, maternal and family health, and population issues. NICHD has established a wide-reaching initiative to generate long-term solutions to childhood obesity. The NICHD website features child health statistics, backgrounders, and many other resources.

Healthy Weight Commitment Foundation

1025 Thomas Jefferson St. NW, Suite 420 E

Washington, DC   20007
(202) 559-7321
e-mail: info@healthyweightcommit.org
website: www.healthyweightcommit.org

The Healthy Weight Commitment Foundation is a national, multiyear effort designed to help reduce obesity, especially childhood obesity. The effort brings together hundreds of retailers, food and beverage manufacturers, restaurants, sporting goods and insurance companies, trade associations, nongovernmental organizations (NGOs), and professional sports organizations. The foundation promotes ways to help people achieve a healthy weight through energy balance. The foundation spearheads initiatives such as the national Together Counts campaign to encourage families to eat meals together. It also provides many resources for students, teachers, families, and communities, such as Energy Balance 101, a free wellness resource.

Let's Move!

website: www.letsmove.gov

Launched by First Lady Michelle Obama in 2010, Let's Move! is a comprehensive initiative dedicated to solving the problem of obesity within a generation. Working in conjunction with the White House Task Force on Child Obesity, Let's Move! has launched a wide variety of programs nationwide in order to promote healthy eating habits, encourage physical activity, provide education about obesity, and more. The Let's Move! website features extensive information and resources about childhood obesity, descriptions of all the various programs enacted under the Let's Move! umbrella, and an interactive map of Let's Move! activities across the country.

Obesity Action Coalition (OAC)

4511 N Himes Ave., Suite 250, Tampa, FL   33614
(800) 717-3117 • fax: (813) 873-7838
website: www.obesityaction.org

The Obesity Action Coalition (OAC) is a national nonprofit organization dedicated to giving a voice to people affected by obesity. The OAC seeks to increase obesity education by offering a wide variety of free educational resources on obesity, morbid obesity, and childhood obesity, in addition to information about the consequences and treatments of these conditions. The OAC also conducts a variety of advocacy efforts throughout the United States on both the national and state levels and encourages individuals to become proactive advocates. The OAC sponsors the Annual Walk from Obesity, which takes place in more than seventy cities across the country each fall. The OAC's *Your Weight Matters* magazine is geared toward those affected by obesity and contains a wide variety of educational and advocacy information.

Partnership for a Healthier America (PHA)

2001 Pennsylvania Ave. NW, Suite 900
Washington, DC   20006
(202) 842-9001
e-mail: info@ahealthieramerica.org
website: www.ahealthieramerica.org

The Partnership for a Healthier America (PHA) is a nonpartisan, nonprofit organization devoted to working with the private sector to ensure the health of the nation's youth by solving the childhood obesity crisis. PHA brings together public, private, and nonprofit leaders to broker meaningful commitments and develop strategies to end childhood obesity. PHA was founded in conjunction with, but is independent from, the Let's Move! campaign. The organization sponsors an annual summit and provides facts about childhood obesity and links to resources provided by Let's Move!

Robert Wood Johnson Foundation (RWJF)

PO Box 2316, Rte. 1 and College Rd. E, Princeton, NJ   08543
(877) 843-7953
website: www.rwjf.org

The mission of the Robert Wood Johnson Foundation (RWJF) is to improve the health and health care of all Americans. The foundation's childhood obesity program seeks to help all children and families eat well and move more, especially those in communities at highest risk for obesity. The foundation's goal is to reverse the childhood obesity epidemic by improving access to affordable healthy foods and increasing opportunities for physical activity in schools and communities across the nation. The RWJF website provides charts and maps detailing obesity in the United States, as well as issue and policy briefs on childhood obesity and obesity in general.

Rudd Center for Food Policy and Obesity
University of Connecticut, One Constitution Plaza, Suite 600
Hartford, CT   06103
(860) 380-1000 • fax: (860) 509-0009
e-mail: rudd.center@uconn.edu
website: www.uconnruddcenter.org

The Rudd Center for Food Policy and Obesity at the University of Connecticut is a nonprofit research and public policy organization devoted to improving the world's diet, preventing obesity, and reducing weight stigma. The center serves as a research institution and clearinghouse for resources that add to the understanding of the complex forces affecting how we eat, how we stigmatize overweight and obese people, and how we can change. The study of food marketing to youth is one of the Rudd Center's core research initiatives. The Rudd Center's monthly newsletter, *Health Digest*, is dedicated to the latest developments in the areas of food policy and obesity.

World Obesity Federation (WOF)
Charles Darwin House, 12 Roger St., London   WCIN 2JU
  UK
+44 20 7685 2580 • fax: +44 20 7685 2581
e-mail: enquiries@worldobesity.org
website: www.worldobesity.org

The World Obesity Federation (WOF) is comprised of professional members of the scientific, medical, and research communities from over fifty obesity associations. The organization is a research-based think tank whose mission is to promote global efforts to reduce, prevent, and treat obesity. The WOF website features extensive information about obesity, including reports and statistics, FAQs, a world map of obesity prevalence, links to external resources, and a special section dedicated to childhood obesity.

Bibliography

Books

Sharon Akabas and Sally Ann Lederman	*Textbook of Obesity: Biological, Psychological and Cultural Influences.* Hoboken, NJ: Wiley-Blackwell, 2012.
Deborah Cohen	*A Big Fat Crisis: The Hidden Forces Behind the Obesity Epidemic—and How We Can End It.* New York: Nation Books, 2015.
Laura Dawes	*Childhood Obesity in America.* Cambridge, MA: Harvard University Press, 2014.
Amy Erdman Farrell	*Fat Shame: Stigma and the Fat Body in American Culture.* New York: NYU Press, 2011.
April Michelle Herndon	*Fat Blame: How the War on Obesity Victimizes Women and Children.* Lawrence: University Press of Kansas, 2014.
Michael Pollan	*The Omnivore's Dilemma: A Natural History of Four Meals.* New York: Penguin, 2007.
Esther Rothblum and Sondra Solovay, eds.	*The Fat Studies Reader.* New York: NYU Press, 2009.
Kristin Voigt and Stuart Nicholls	*Childhood Obesity: Ethical and Policy Issues.* Oxford, United Kingdom: Oxford University Press, 2014.

Marilyn Wann   *FAT!SO?: Because You Don't Have to Apologize for Your Size.* Berkeley, CA: Ten Speed Press, 1998.

Jacob Warren and   *Always the Fat Kid—The Truth About* K. Bryant Smalley   *the Enduring Effects of Childhood Obesity.* New York: Palgrave Macmillan, 2013.

Rebecca Jane   *Fat Kids: Truth and Consequences.* Weinstein   New York: Beaufort Books, 2014.

Periodicals and Internet Sources

Associated Press   "Puerto Rico Considers Fining Parents of Obese Children," myfoxny.com, February 10, 2015. www.fox5ny.com.

Ameena Batada   "Kids' Meals II: Obesity and Poor Nutrition on the Menu," Center for Science in the Public Interest, 2013. www.cspinet.org.

Luke Beckmann   "Parents, Not Government, Know How to Feed Their Children," *The Daily Signal*, August 8, 2013. http://dailysignal.com.

Roy Bergold Jr.   "Is Obesity Really Our Fault?," *QSR Magazine*, June 2010.

Laura Bult and   "NYC Board of Health's New, Stricter Jennifer Fermino   Rules for Day Cares Limit How Much Juice Kids Can Drink, Cut 'Sedentary' Time," *New York Daily News*, March 23, 2015.

California Department of Public Health   "Obesity in California: The Weight of the State, 2000–2012," 2014. www.cdph.ca.gov.

Hank Cardello   "How the Food Industry Can Solve Our Childhood Obesity Crisis," *The Atlantic*, December 13, 2011.

Hank Cardello   "Why Big Food Belongs in the School Lunchroom," *Forbes*, September 4, 2014.

Alicia Chang   "Study: Fast-Food Limits Didn't Cut Obesity Rate in South LA," Associated Press, March 19, 2015. http://hosted.ap.org.

Shin-Yi Chou, Inas Rashad, and Michael Grossman   "Fast-Food Restaurant Advertising on Television and Its Influence on Childhood Obesity," *Journal of Law and Economics*, November 2008.

KJ Dell'Antonia   "Parents Don't Notice Extra Pounds on Overweight Children," *New York Times*, May 20, 2015. http://parenting.blogs.nytimes.com.

Thomas DiNapoli   "Soaring Health Care Costs Highlight Need to Address Childhood Obesity," Office of the NY State Comptroller, October 2012. http://osc.state.ny.us.

Eric Andrew Finkelstein, Wan Chen Kang Graham, and Rahul Malhotra   "Lifetime Direct Medical Costs of Childhood Obesity," *Pediatrics*, February 7, 2014.

Food Research and Action Center — "Hunger and Obesity? Making the Connections," 2010. www.frac.org.

Christina Gresh — "The Epidemic of Childhood Obesity," *Reporter*, September 19, 2013.

Tom Hamburger — "Michelle Obama's School Lunch Agenda Faces Backlash from Some School Nutrition Officials," *Washington Post*, May 30, 2014.

Elizabeth Harrington — "Feds to Weigh Children in Daycare," *Washington Free Beacon*, March 20, 2015.

Elizabeth Harrington — "Second Grader Buckles Under Pressure from White House," *Washington Free Beacon*, March 6, 2015.

Jennifer Harris et al. — "Fast Food FACTS 2013: Measuring Progress in Nutrition and Marketing to Children and Teens," Yale Rudd Center for Food Policy and Obesity, 2013. http://fastfoodmarketing.org.

Healthy Eating Research — "Recommendations for Responsible Food Marketing to Children," January 2015. http://healthyeatingresearch.org.

Michelle Healy — "Price Tag for Childhood Obesity: $19,000 per Kid," *USA Today*, April 7, 2014. www.usatoday.com.

William Hudson   "For Schoolchildren, Where's the Water?," CNN, April 18, 2011. www.cnn.com.

Sameera Karnik and Amar Kanekar   "Childhood Obesity: A Global Public Health Crisis," *International Journal of Preventive Medicine*, January 2012.

The kNOw Youth Media   "Parents Are Responsible for Health of Children," May 25, 2013. www.theknowfresno.org.

Jeffrey Levi et al.   "F as in Fat: How Obesity Threatens America's Future," Trust for America's Health and Robert Wood Johnson Foundation, 2012. www.rwjf.org.

Jeffrey Levi et al.   "The State of Obesity: Better Policies for a Healthier America 2014," Trust for America's Health and Robert Wood Johnson Foundation, September 2014. www.rwjf.org.

Anastasia Moloney and Chris Arsenault   "Obesity Weighs on Latin America After Success in Fight Against Hunger," Reuters, February 13, 2015. http://ca.news.yahoo.com.

New York Times   "Driving Down Childhood Obesity" (editorial), February 27, 2014.

Mandy Oaklander   "Antibiotics Before Age 2 Increase Risk of Childhood Obesity," *Time*, September 29, 2014.

Obesity Society   "Childhood Overweight," 2015. www.obesity.org.

Carroll Ogden et al.

"Prevalence of Childhood and Adult Obesity in the United States, 2011–2012," *Journal of the American Medical Association*, February 26, 2014.

Kim Painter

"No Real Progress on Child Obesity, Latest Report Says," *USA Today*, April 7, 2014.

Tara Parker-Pope

"The Fat Trap," *New York Times*, December 28, 2011.

Tom Philpott

"Conservatives Bravely Defend Kids' Right to Junky Lunch," *Mother Jones*, October 17, 2012.

Physician's Committee for Responsible Medicine

"Childhood Lost: How the Happy Meal Can Lead to Diabetes, Obesity, and Hypertension," 2014. www.pcrm.org.

Jennifer M. Poti, Kiyah J. Duffey, and Barry M. Popkin

"The Association of Fast Food Consumption with Poor Dietary Outcomes and Obesity Among Children: Is It the Fast Food or the Remainder of the Diet?," *American Journal of Clinical Nutrition*, January 2014.

Poncie Rutsch

"Is It Time For a Warning Label on Sugar-Loaded Drinks?," National Public Radio, April 9, 2015. www.npr.org.

Andrew Seaman "US Childhood Obesity Rates Have Actually Increased Over the Past 14 Years (STUDY)," *Huffington Post*, April 8, 2014. www.huffingtonpost.com.

Christopher Snowdon "The Slippery Slope of Food Regulations," *Cato Unbound*, January 27, 2015. www.cato-unbound.org.

Sabrina Tavernise "Obesity Rate for Young Children Plummets 43% in a Decade," *New York Times*, 2014.

Joseph Thompson "Testimony Before the Senate Health, Education, Labor and Pensions Committee: Childhood Obesity: Beginning the Dialogue on Reversing the Epidemic," March 4, 2010. www.help.senate.gov.

University of North Carolina at Chapel Hill "Fast Food Not the Major Cause of Rising Childhood Obesity Rates, Study Finds," *ScienceDaily*, January 2014. www.sciencedaily.com.

Elizabeth Siris Winchester "Childhood Obesity: A Growing Problem," *Childhood Obesity Prevention* (blog), January 29, 2013. www.childhoodobesitydeerpark.com.

Amy Winterfeld, Douglas Shinkle, and Larry Morandi "State Actions to Promote Healthy Communities and Prevent Childhood Obesity, 2012," National Conference of State Legislatures, 2013. www.ncsl.org.

Josh Zembik   "Blumenthal, Harkin Introduce Bill
                   to End Federal Tax Subsidy for
                   Unhealthy Food, Beverage Marketing
                   to Children," blumenthal.senate.gov,
                   May 15, 2014. www.blumenthal
                   .senate.gov.

Index